The Politics of Life

# The Politics of Life

*25 Rules for Survival*
*in a Brutal and*
*Manipulative*
*World*

CRAIG CRAWFORD

ROWMAN & LITTLEFIELD PUBLISHERS, INC.
*Lanham · Boulder · New York · Toronto · Plymouth, UK*

ROWMAN & LITTLEFIELD PUBLISHERS, INC.

Published in the United States of America
by Rowman & Littlefield Publishers, Inc.
A wholly owned subsidiary of The Rowman & Littlefield Publishing Group, Inc.
4501 Forbes Boulevard, Suite 200, Lanham, Maryland 20706
www.rowmanlittlefield.com

Estover Road
Plymouth PL6 7PY
United Kingdom

Distributed by National Book Network

British Library Cataloguing in Publication Information Available

**Library of Congress Cataloging-in-Publication Data**
The hardback edition of this book was previously cataloged
by the Library of Congress as follows:

Crawford, Craig, 1956-
The politics of life : 25 rules for survival in a brutal and
manipulative world / Craig Crawford.
p. cm.
Includes index.
1. Conduct of life. I. Title.
BJ1521.C73 2007
158.2—dc22                                      2006034664

ISBN: 978-0-7425-5250-0 (cloth : alk. paper)
ISBN: 978-0-7425-5251-7 (pbk : alk. paper)
ISBN: 978-0-4422-1297-8 (electronic)

Printed in the United States of America

⊚™ The paper used in this publication meets the minimum requirements
of American National Standard for Information Sciences—Permanence
of Paper for Printed Library Materials, ANSI/NISO Z39.48-1992.

*Dedicated to my editor, David Blank, for his
keen eye and gentle ways;*

*to my agent, Diane Nine, for nudging me forward;*

*to my parents, Bill and Toby, for their
patience and courage; and*

*to the kind and generous people of
Lost River, West Virginia, for knowing exactly
how to treat a struggling writer.*

# Contents

*Foreword* · ix

*Introduction* · xv

RULE 1 Life Is a Filthy Battle for Control · 1

RULE 2 Better to Boldly Assert Than Cautiously Deny · 8

RULE 3 Love Helps, but Fear Motivates · 13

RULE 4 Popular Lies Beat Unpopular Truth · 19

RULE 5 Ambition Is Never Satisfied · 25

RULE 6 Only the Flexible Succeed · 31

RULE 7 Better to Imitate a Winner Than Be
an Original Loser · 37

RULE 8 Never Keep Your Word If Circumstances Change · 43

RULE 9 To Control Others, First Walk in Their Shoes · 49

RULE 10 The More Visible Your Power, the More Its
Limits Are Known · 55

RULE 11 Arrogance Makes an Easy Target · 62

RULE 12 Most Would Rather Follow a Leader Than
Lead a Following · 69

RULE 13 Those Who Prefer to Lead a Following
Cannot Be Trusted · 75

## Contents

RULE 14   Never Seek a Favor That Could Cost Too Much to Return · 81

RULE 15   Leading the Way for Change Seldom Pays · 87

RULE 16   Wanting Power Requires Less Intelligence Than Seeking Power · 94

RULE 17   Those Who Are Dependent on You Will Be the Most Faithful · 100

RULE 18   A True Enemy Should Be Eliminated, Never Tolerated · 107

RULE 19   In Dealing with Passive Aggression, Be More Passive and More Aggressive · 113

RULE 20   Victory Can Sometimes Be Concealed in Compromise · 120

RULE 21   Implement Painful Choices Quickly to Minimize the Effects · 126

RULE 22   Distribute Rewards Slowly to Prolong the Effects · 132

RULE 23   Allowing Others to Speak Truthfully Diminishes Their Respect for You · 138

RULE 24   Never Postpone Inevitable Conflict · 144

RULE 25   The Powerful Never Give Up Control; It Must Be Taken Away · 150

*Index* · 157

*About the Author* · 165

**To: President Barack Obama**
**From: "Niccolo Machiavelli"**

Upon the occasion of your plans for another term in office, Mr. President, and wishing now myself to offer some proof of my admiration for this fine book of rules based upon my own writings nearly five centuries ago, I present here my estimation of your political skills.

As I wrote in the dedication to my book of instruction, *The Prince*, I have found "nothing amongst all I possess that I hold more dear or esteem more highly than the knowledge of the actions of great men, which I have acquired by long experience of modern affairs and a continued study of ancient history."

I maintain no quarrel with the essential rules for the common man crafted in Mr. Crawford's book, *The Politics of Life*, and naturally I am flattered by my devoted student's many references to my works. But unlike him, my own meditations on the subject of power exclusively attend to those who hold or seek control of the seats of government.

Still, I applaud Mr. Crawford's guide to the practice of politics for those of more humble station, from those who find themselves in need of defense against manipulative foes in their place of work to those who face the many challenges of gaining power over a variety of situations or persons. And he has done so, as was always my aim, without pomposity or resort to high-sounding and magnificent words, nor with any other allurements or extrinsic embellishments.

Now, to the task at hand.

Mr. President, while a preponderance of the 25 rules in *The Politics of Life* apply to the arc of your early years in office, I have settled upon three that seem especially apt. While some of my observations are more cautionary than complimentary, it must first be said that anyone who gains control of the loftiest political office in the world's most powerful nation is by definition a skilled practioner of the art.

You are to be congratulated for your initial success. However, for your continued success in the great challenge of holding and wielding power, a few adjustments might be in order.

## "NEVER KEEP YOUR WORD IF CIRCUMSTANCES CHANGE"

In his eighth rule within, Mr. Crawford rightly notes that "shifting stance without getting caught is one of the most difficult strokes in the art of politics." And he was most generous in citing my own thought on the matter: "A prudent ruler cannot, and must not, honor his word when it places him at a disadvantage and when the reasons for which he made his promise no longer exist."

Mr. President, you have shown a keen understanding of this reality and a willingness to try. In matters of war and social change you often chose not to meet the full measure of your campaign promises, or, when attempting to keep some promises you did so in such a halting manner that many of your most ardent supporters became impatient.

You suffer from a lack of nimbleness in the ways of applying this rule that maximize the cost to your image. In other words, as Mr. Crawford might say in the vernacular of his 21st Century tongue, you "get caught too much."

Perhaps a fitting model for improvement would be one of your predecessors, President William Clinton—or "Bill," as I believe he allowed himself to be all too familiarly called. This remarkably talented politician often shifted stance while minimizing cost by applying a succinct formula that Mr. Crawford details in this chapter:

Acknowledge that you made a promise that must be broken. Pretending that you kept a promise you have broken only complicates your political predicament. Apologize profusely. And make a convincing case for how the changing circumstances causing you to break your word were unforeseeable when you made the promise. Most importantly, develop compelling reasons for why breaking the promise actually benefits those to whom you had made it.


## "Leading the Way for Change Seldom Pays"

Here, Mr. President, you have learned Mr. Crawford's fifteenth rule the hard way. Having come to power on the rising tide of populist desire to unsettle the powerful, it was inevitable that you would be forced to disillusion such unreasonable expectations.

As Mr. Crawford observes in this chapter, on most occasions variation is more achievable than far-reaching change.

"Change is upsetting and repetition is tedious," he writes. "But give people some variety between the two extremes, and they are more likely to follow your lead."

Of course, there will be those among your subjects who unreasonably demand radical change and turn against you if it is not achieved. The balance a political leader must seek is to make enough alterations to keep the moderate minded content enough so as to prevent radical forces from leveraging any significant claim to your power.

When you set upon a course of real change, as you have done in some instances Mr. President, there are certain techniques to follow. Never spring ill-formed ideas upon the public. Acknowledge and seek to undermine the tactical advantages that keepers of the status quo always enjoy. Control the conversation before anger and resistance overwhelm you.

Change is often alluring to the citizens of any regime, but in stable societies it can be less desirable to the people than they themselves might think once it is actually attempted. Generally in the politics of governing a state that is not in actual danger of being overthrown, dramatic change is best deployed mostly as a rhetorical device.

## "Never Postpone Inevitable Conflict"

In the twenty-fourth rule below we find reasoned advice that might serve you well, Mr. President. Perhaps attributable to the uncertainty that accompanies any new job your first term was often marked by a tendency to allow political foes to flourish without adequate confrontation, publicly or privately.

By not severely and consistently applying the pressure that the powers of your status can provide, a leader finds himself agreeing to more compromises than necessary. In worst case scenarios the leader becomes the follower.

The intransigence of many political office holders who oppose you clearly shows that on quite a few matters conflict is simply inevitable. Postponing that conflict, or failing to at least clarify which stands you will not yield in negotiation, serves to empower the other side.

In governing, whether on domestic or foreign issues, your willingness to concede is constantly being tested. Still, it is also unwise to invite conflict that is avoidable and not beneficial to your interests, or to adopt an unyielding stance without the will or ability to maintain it.

As Mr. Crawford plainly recommends in this chapter: "Try not to shoot at anything that can shoot back. But do not hesitate to shoot if you are about to get shot."

*Niccolo Machiavelli (1469-1527) was an Italian philosopher, diplomat, playwright and civil servant based in Florence during the Renaissance. He is considered to have been one of the founders of modern political science*

# INTRODUCTION

*It seems to me better to represent things as they are*
*in actual truth, rather than as they are imagined.*
NICCOLO MACHIAVELLI

These are the twenty-five rules for surviving the politics of everyday life. While applying to professional politicians, they are not just for those who run governments and not just for "civilians" in the commonplace world who are seeking to manipulate others. They are also for the laid-back and easygoing among us who need help dealing with a bully, a boss, a coworker, or a family member who is trying to control your life to his or her own ends or otherwise make you miserable in one of the many ways that a skilled political operator can do.

Wherever humans are found, there is politics. The human being is nature's top predator. As such, we prey for control. Whether inventing umbrellas to control the effects of nature or bombing nations to subdue them, we never stop seeking control. Even driving our car presents a series of roving battles and negotiations to control and defend our space, the essence of politics.

Even if you prefer to live in denial and tell yourself that you are above it all, you will not get too far in life without learning how to deal with those who are not. You might consider this a course in self-defense.

These rules are inspired by principles of Niccolo Machiavelli, a sixteenth-century philosopher and historian whose book *The Prince* became the bible for politicians through generations since. Machiavelli's keen eye for human behavior is matched with the secrets and strategies of master politicians throughout history, applying the lessons of their experiences to ordinary life.

So many of us say that we hate politics, but it rules our lives more than we think. Whether maneuvering for a better table at a restaurant or pushing for a promotion, we deploy political tactics for control and success.

Watching real people play politics made a television-ratings hit of the CBS show *Survivor* at the start of the twenty-first century. Stranded on a deserted island, the contestants formed coalitions to vote other members off of the island until only the last survivor remained. Not surprisingly, the winner in each series of this fascinating show turned out to be the most skilled politician.

*Survivor* spawned many copycat shows, and nearly all of them featured humans playing politics in one way or another. Reality-based television would appeal to Machiavelli. After all, he is considered to be one of the world's first reality-based historians, coming along at a time when others in his line of work strove to please the powerful with mythological and often fraudulent renditions of their great works and goodness. Machiavelli would have none of that. He sought the truth about how the powerful really get control—and keep it. "It seems to me better to represent things as they are in actual truth, rather than as they are imagined," Machiavelli wrote.

Be warned that the "actual truth" of these rules will at times seem harsh and cruel, perhaps even immoral. But that is what comes with the turf when you are learning to deal with others as they actually behave, not how "they are imagined." There are other books for telling us how we ought to be. Here, we only examine what is.

Think again about driving your car and how people actually behave on the roads. While plenty of drivers are kind and generous, many are rude, obnoxious, and even threatening. No matter how they act elsewhere, remember this: What you see on the road is who they really are. You could be at a party with those same rude drivers, and they might put up a gentle and affable front. But in the anonymous bubble of their automobiles, they are their true selves.

These rules are meant to help you identify and reckon with the "true selves" of the people around you. Unavoidably, it also serves as a manual for the Machiavellians out there who want to manipulate the world to suit their needs.

Politics repels and entertains us. Jay Leno seldom does a *Tonight Show* monologue without a joke or two about politicians. Many of the rules that follow might repel you. Ideally, some will entertain you.

We can deny these rules, as we often do, but ultimately they describe life as a human in "actual truth."

## Life Is a Filthy Battle for Control

*A dictatorship would be a heck of a lot easier.*
PRESIDENT GEORGE W. BUSH

We begin the battle for control on the day that we are born. As babies, we quickly learn to cry for food and attention. When it comes to seeking control, some people never really grow up. Sure, their techniques become more sophisticated, but no matter how skilled at hiding it, many adults are still just babies crying for attention.

Control is our most basic need at birth and beyond. To feed their appetites, ego, and ambition, most people must control others. Life is a filthy battle for control.

It never stops. I once got into a stupid argument with a cab driver and later realized just how poorly I had handled the situation—all because I was trying to control the situation. And so was he.

When two controlling humans collide, watch out. So often, when emotions cool and you ask yourself a simple question, you come to see just how unnecessary the dispute had been. Just ask, "What were we really arguing about?"

I had to laugh when I honestly and fundamentally answered that question about my hostilities with the cab driver.

We were arguing about why he came early to pick me up for a ride to the airport. Why on earth would I get angry about something like that? It was all about control, and it had nothing to do with the substance of our differences—which, upon reflection, turned out to be not so real at all.

You see, I wanted to control what time he picked me up, and he wanted to control how I ordered cabs from his company. He said that I had to call at least two hours ahead to arrange a specific time for pickup. I had called thirty minutes before the time I wanted to leave. When he arrived within the next fifteen minutes of my call, I was not ready. He called twice, and I told him that I was not ready. By the time I came out—at the exact time that I had originally wanted to get in a cab—he was all flustered, complaining that I was late and threatening to charge extra.

I stormed off, could not find another cab, and missed my plane—which made me the loser in this ridiculous episode. Control, once achieved, often has a way of being a disappointment. There is a simple reason. Ultimately, control is unachievable and, in the end, not always worth seeking. Had I let the driver have control, and agreed to follow his company's procedures, I would have gotten to the airport on time.

## Sometimes You Can Be Content without Control

Even when we think we have control, those whom we think that we are controlling might actually have the upper hand. They always have the power to reject your control, unless you have them locked up in the basement. The controller does not have a choice in the matter if the need for control is powerful enough.

The need for control varies. For many, it is a simple need. "When neither their property nor their honor is touched, the majority live content," Machiavelli wrote.

Sometimes I think that the most powerful people on the planet are those who seem to be content without micromanaging everyone around them. We say that they are "comfortable in their own skin." This means that they do not have to live in somebody else's skin to be content.

"Blessed are the meek," Jesus said. How true. In my life's journey I have found that those rare people who never seek to control others are almost always the happiest. They generally have less money and virtually no power, but blessed are those who require neither. You might think that control makes you happy, but try giving up control for a time and see if you still think so.

Most of us fall somewhere between the bliss of never needing control and the angst of always seeking it. The first step to managing control is to understand where we fit into that range. And if you do not like where you fit, you are on the way to making adjustments—because now you are self-aware, a critical juncture in developing the right mix of tools for playing and surviving the politics of life in the human race.

Introspection does not come easy to many people. Even the self-obsessed often cannot honestly look at themselves. But doing so is vital to making your way in the world. A leading American sociologist, Charles Horton Cooley, believed in what he called the "looking-glass self" as a tool for developing the capacity to reflect upon your own behavior.

He offered three simple steps that can be a useful start for examining control issues:

1. To begin, picture how you see your own appearance, your traits and personalities.

2. Then, picture how others react to you and interpret those reactions to visualize how you think that they really see you.

3. Develop your own self-concept, based not only on how you see yourself, but on how you interpret and visualize the reactions of other people.

## Politics Is the Art of Control

Those who need total control we call "control freaks." There is always one somewhere—at work, at school, or just driving down the highway. Whether you are a control freak needing to break the addiction or are someone at the mercy of one, learning to understand the basics of control is a useful journey.

However much control we need, the techniques for getting it are constant. The rest of this book explores those techniques. For most of us, our control skills rarely advance beyond the crude efforts of our infancy.

We often mistake power for control. Power is a means for control. Using power to force others to our will is effective but not lasting. Relying on raw power leaves us out of control when the power is inevitably gone.

Overbearing parents who rely only on their absolute power to control a child's behavior eventually lose control as their power fades when the dependent child becomes an independent adult. Since we seldom have absolute power over others, how do we gain control and get what we want? We play politics, the process of making others want what we want so that everybody wins. Using political skill to encourage children or employees to want to behave in a certain way wins lasting control over them more effectively than using absolute power to order them to do so.

Politics is the art of control. More difficult and ultimately more rewarding than absolute power, playing politics depends on shaping the wants and needs of others to achieve our own desires.

No matter how unskilled, we as human beings play politics, manipulating others to our own ends. At the office, we seek control of the boss and our colleagues in the hopes of winning a raise, a promotion, or a better desk. At home, we seek control of our family members, to shape our children in our own image; to persuade our parents to give us money; or to gain the love, affection, and attention our ego requires.

In society, we are always playing politics for control. We enter a restaurant looking for the best table, plotting how to maneuver the headwaiter to get us there. Even driving our cars can be a frustrating political battle to control the roads for the quickest or safest journey. Few of us carefully devise successful strategies for achieving our goals, small or large. We clumsily demand the better table or lean on the car horn to bully another driver—behavior that might work on occasion but takes us no further than wailing for a bottle as a newborn.

Playing politics to win control of others requires a mastery of technique no less rigorous than how the finest athletes train their bodies for competition. Understanding strategy is as vital in political play as it is on the baseball field. The political player must intensely study others, identifying their motives and meeting their needs to gain control of their behavior.

Even those who think that they have no need to control others must protect themselves by learning to identify and respond to those who do. You might be the most content worker with no ambition other than maintaining your status quo. But without a keen awareness of political rules, you could lose your happy place to an ambitious colleague whose motives and techniques you saw too late.

Masterful politicians are the most advanced among us in the art of control. Their words and deeds are consciously crafted to control the behavior of individuals and the masses. Political skill can be dangerous, for it exists apart from ideology. The control that it delivers can be used for good or evil. In the same era, Winston Churchill and Adolph Hitler used their command of political rhetoric and symbols to motivate a mass of followers toward opposite ends.

We choose how we use the control that our political skills deliver. But whether we use it solely to become rich and famous or whether we use it to better humanity, the rules of winning control are the same.

## Everyone Wants to Be a Dictator

George W. Bush was joking when he said that "a dictatorship would be a heck of a lot easier"—or so we thought. He made the remark to the press corps early in his presidency when asked about how he would deal with Congress. He might have been kidding around, but Congress, despite being controlled by Bush's political party, the Republicans, ended up in countless battles with his administration over his seemingly insatiable desire to subdue the legislative branch and dramatically expand the power of the presidency.

But did that make life easier for Bush? Certainly not in his second term, when Congress nixed most of his agenda, largely because he had so persistently sought control so much so that those he wished to dominate finally balked, leaving him politically isolated. This is how things usually end up for those who exclusively demand control but ignore the complex nuances of playing a skillful game of politics to achieve it.

# Better to Boldly Assert Than Cautiously Deny

*When you come to a fork in the road, take it.*
Yogi Berra

When first accused of having an affair with a young intern while president, Bill Clinton did something that was later deemed a terrible mistake. He lied. It was not a mistake.

At a televised press conference shortly after the first reports of his affair with Monica Lewinsky, the president sternly asserted that he had not had an affair with "that woman." In a television interview, First Lady Hillary Clinton accused a "vast right-wing conspiracy" of spreading the story.

The president lied, with his wife as a knowing or unknowing accomplice. Later, the lie was compounded in grand jury testimony, leading to his impeachment in the House and to a Senate trial where he escaped ouster from office.

Although his original lie caused Clinton a world of legal trouble, it also saved his presidency. When faced with the revelations of his Lewinsky relations, Clinton wisely pondered the mood of the public. He asked a top aide whether the public was ready for their president to admit the affair. They concluded that in time Americans would absorb the story and put it into a context that would not force him from office.

Clinton chose to boldly assert his innocence, maintaining adequate support in public opinion polls for many months. By the time that Clinton publicly admitted the Lewinsky affair, most Americans told pollsters that they believed it was true but did not think that he should leave office for it.

Had Clinton been honest in the beginning, he might have avoided the legal morass that followed, but his public support would have plummeted at a time when leaders of his own party were grumbling that he should resign.

While few of us would ever face a Senate impeachment trial as a consequence of our decisions, Clinton's experience is not so far from regular life.

An eighteenth-century American politician, Aaron Burr, once said that the job of a lawyer is to "boldly assert and plausibly maintain." It is a workable plan not just for lawyers. People often get their way simply by asserting something, whether or not it is true, so long as they come up with believable-sounding support for their position. Such confidence and skill tend to attract followers even if the assertion is a big lie.

Equivocation, no matter how honest or justified, is seen as weakness. If asked a question at an important meeting, the bold assertion of an uncertain answer in a firm, steady voice will yield better results than will a meekly stated certain fact.

In Clinton's case, many Americans admired his stubborn denials, even if they did not believe him. His bold assertion helped him politically survive without making his claim as believable as Burr advised.

## CAUTIOUS DENIALS MAKE
## YOU LOOK WEAK

Cautious denials breed suspicion. Not only will people think that you are lying, but they will not respect you. It makes you look weak.

Let's say that you are a manager of a business and are planning for the possibility of massive layoffs. How do you answer the question about the chance of layoffs when it comes up in a meeting with employees and you are not quite ready to spill the beans? The worst response for employee morale is to admit that you might or might not lay off employees but cannot really say for sure at this time. This might be the truth but is probably a disaster to say so. A weak equivocation fuels gossip and allows imaginations to run wild. The better response is to forcefully declare your determination to avoid layoffs and detail the steps that all employees can take to help you in this cause.

Sometimes it does not hurt to be brutally blunt. At a company where I once worked, the top executive took questions from the assembled crowd of employees who were worried about rumored layoffs. He vowed to avoid such pain but gave no ground on the dire straits that we faced. And when a worker began pestering him about losing some perks to cutbacks, the executive plainly said, "Your job is your perk." There was much gnashing of teeth among the workers after hearing the remark, but the message got across: Quit your whining and be glad you have a job.

Another approach is to boldly deny the facts, as Clinton did, and slowly prepare the way for hard truths to come out on your own terms.

## The Appearance of Weakness Can Be
## an Effective Tool for Control

There are times when the seemingly weak get their way. My mother has been known to shed a tear or two to get something done. Once, when I was about eleven years old, we were stuck in an airport and all but abandoned by the airline that had overbooked the flight, leaving about a dozen angry passengers with nothing to do but yell at the airline staff.

My mother followed a different path. She cornered one of the airline workers and began crying, clutching me at her side as if I were a wayward orphan. The man took pity, ushered us into a VIP room, and got us first-class seats on the flight. We quietly walked past the angry mob, and as far as I know, we were the only ones in the group to make the flight.

Some might find it a bit much to break out tears to control others, but there are cases when revealing a bit of vulnerability can restart a situation that is spinning out of your control. Famous people often resort to the weakness defense when they get into trouble. Movie actor Mel Gibson tried this gambit when he was arrested for drunk driving and officers quoted him verbally attacking Jews in his alcohol-induced stupor. Shortly afterward, he began releasing statements appealing to Jewish leaders for help in his need for recovery.

People are generally forgiving and often respond positively to those who admit their mistakes and seek help, no matter how disingenuous those pleas might be. But it is a card that should be played judiciously. Consider it a last resort.

Playing the victim or martyr too often can be disastrous. Prizefighter Mike Tyson got plenty of sympathy the first few times he made an ass of himself. But once he chewed off a chunk of somebody's ear, he had run his course for public empathy.

## Choosing Your Fork

Yogi Berra is a legend for quotes that make sense on a gut level, though not necessarily on a literal level. One of his classics—"When you come to a fork in the road, take it"— strikes me as profoundly good advice. Hardly as lyrical as Robert Frost's "Two roads diverge in a yellow wood," Berra's clumsy words suggest an important life lesson: Do something! People admire action. They dislike indecision, even if they bitterly complain about the choices that you make.

## Love Helps, but Fear Motivates

*Once they feel the heat, they'll see the light.*
LYNDON JOHNSON

Getting others to do what we want can be life's greatest challenge. Which is better? A carrot or a stick? The answer is both.

Fear motivates. Children behave best if they fear punishment. Employees work harder if they fear for their jobs. But control depends on instilling both fear and love in others. It as all about finding the right balance. Too much fear produces hatred. Too much love can lead to disrespect.

When Richard Nixon took power after a decade of struggling for the White House, he assembled such a fierce band of tough guys around him that his reign was famously dubbed the Imperial Presidency. Political foes, members of Congress, the media, and anyone else who challenged them faced threats, intimidation, and surveillance. A top Nixon aide, Charles Colson, summed up his boss's style when he said, "Grab their balls, and their hearts and minds will follow."

While Nixon's leadership by fear quickly made him one of the most powerful presidents in modern times, it was also his undoing. When investigations of the White House role in the

Watergate break-in left Nixon vulnerable, the many enemies he once intimidated were only too eager to bring him down.

Nixon violated one of Machiavelli's central rules for rulers: Instill fear, but not so much so that you instill hatred. Had Nixon made more lasting friendships in Congress, he might have found a safety net when he needed it most.

Machiavelli distrusted love as a leader's sole tool in motivating others because he believed that it shifts too much control to the loved one. "When you are hard pressed, they turn away," he wrote. Fear persists as a motivator, Machiavelli believed, because the leader controls its cause: "Fear is sustained by a dread of punishment that is always effective."

Still, Machiavelli advocated using both fear and love to control others (when both are possible), arguing that the super leader finds a balance between the two and reaches a state of popular goodwill by unifying coercion and popular consent.

## REWARDS CREATE PASSIVE FEAR

How do you have it both ways, using love and fear to motivate? Use a reward system—positive reinforcement, as the psychologists call it.

Rewards create passive fear—a fear of not getting further rewards. Rewards give you control of the cause of the behavior that you seek. Rewards (obviously) do not create hatred. Buy a friend dinner for helping move your furniture, and you might condition this friend to seek your favor. Casual Friday at the office is a subtle control mechanism delivered as a reward. By allowing employees the choice of wearing casual clothes on a particular day, employers please workers while reminding them who controls the dress code.

American presidents often try to cut taxes early in their administration, an effective way to assert control in a positive manner. Among those who put it to good use: John F. Kennedy, Ronald Reagan, and George W. Bush.

We don't all have to issue checks to every American taxpayer to apply this rule. Even the smallest gestures can create an emotional bond that gives us control of the relationship: a personal thank-you note to a party host, a bottle of your boss's favorite wine at Christmas, or a word of praise to a coworker for a job well done.

What if Nixon had collected a lifetime of goodwill for small gestures with those who eventually brought him down? It was not his partisan enemies but his Republican Party colleagues who pulled the final plug. When a group of GOP politicians led by Senator Barry Goldwater of Arizona called on Nixon to resign, he lost any chance of staying in office.

A personal bond based on respect and friendship yields maximum control, as it might have saved Nixon's relationship with his own party leaders. Nixon stands in history as a monument to going too far with Machiavelli's advice to rule by fear. Machiavelli preferred motivating by fear, but only if necessary. In the end he urged the balanced approach: "My view is that it is desirable to be both loved and feared."

## THE POLITICS OF FEAR

For understanding the limitless powers of fear, there is nothing like politics in America after the September 11, 2001, terrorist attacks. The mostly deadly assault on U.S. soil in history created a climate of fear like none since the Great Depression.

But George W. Bush handled the threat of terror quite differently from the way that Franklin Roosevelt responded to economic tragedy. Bush used fear to his advantage; Roosevelt rallied Americans to fight their fears.

After the 2001 al Qaeda attacks on New York and the Pentagon, the Bush administration skillfully played the fear card against domestic political foes, often raising terror alerts at politically opportune moments. In the summer of 2004, during the president's reelection campaign, the White House even went so far as to herald what turned out to be badly outdated terror threats during the Democratic Party convention in Boston, where John Kerry was formally nominated for president.

Bush's campaign guru, Karl Rove, repeatedly advised fellow Republicans to blast opponents as unfit to protect the nation. He summed it up as a difference in worldviews. "Republicans have a post-9/11 worldview, and many Democrats have a pre-9/11 worldview," he said in a speech to the Republican National Committee before the 2006 congressional elections. "That doesn't make them unpatriotic—not at all. But it does make them wrong—deeply and profoundly and consistently wrong."

Rove might not put it this blatantly in a campaign brochure. But you could sum up his political battle plan with a simple phrase: Fear trumps all. Contrast this approach with Roosevelt's signature comfort line, "We have nothing to fear but fear itself."

Bush greatly enhanced his political power with the fear motivator, bypassing laws intended to restrict federal eavesdropping and jumping legal hurdles in the detainment of war prisoners that even the U.S. Supreme Court, although dominated by Republican appointees, ultimately balked at allowing.

The Bush war on terror is too close in time at this writing to accurately assess its pluses and minuses, but my guess is that he overplayed the fear card. Instead of calling the nation to action, Bush repeatedly told Americans to go about their normal lives and trust him to protect them from the "evil ones."

There is a danger to democracy in persuading people to indulge their fears and trade liberty for safety—especially so in an amorphous war against terror that might not end for a generation or longer. The longer the war, the more lasting the loss of liberty, shifting great and irretrievable power to those in charge.

The potential consequences of a perpetual U.S. war against terror recalls George Orwell's cautionary tale in his political novel *1984*. He described a nation always at war against anonymous foes and the expansive political power it conferred on that nation's rulers. Attributing slogans such as "war is peace" to his fictional leaders, Orwell extensively examined how politicians in the real world can subdue their subjects with the effective use of fear.

## From Heat to Light

Few presidents in American history carried the big stick quite like Lyndon Johnson did, even though Teddy Roosevelt first popularized that image to describe the nation's emerging influence around the world. Turning up the heat, Johnson once noted, often makes people "see the light."

While Johnson used this approach to win historic victories for his legislative agenda in Congress, from the Civil

Rights Act to his Great Society antipoverty programs, those of us with lesser agendas can turn up the heat to great effect as well.

Of course, one must *have* a stick to use it on another. Threats without at least the appearance of the means for punishment are unlikely to get results. And even Johnson did not forget the carrot, rewarding politicians who submitted to his will with generous federal spending in their home states.

It sounds harsh, but manipulating people to your will is not unlike training dogs. As a kid, I watched my father alternate strategies to train hunting dogs. Sometimes a rolled-up newspaper rapped across the nose was a necessary tool for getting their attention or shedding them of a bad habit. At other times he gave them love and attention to reward good behavior. Give too much of one or the other, and you will end up with a useless dog.

## Popular Lies Beat Unpopular Truth

*If one tells the truth, one is sure*
*sooner or later to be found out.*
OSCAR WILDE

In Jerzy Kosinski's hilariously haunting novel *Being There*, a simple-minded gardener becomes a national hero and presidential adviser with empty headed phrases that he means to apply to only his gardening. "There will be growth in the spring," he tells a grateful nation during bad economic times, sending his president's popularity soaring despite referring to only his garden, not the fate of the economy.

The premise of Kosinski's character, expertly played by Peter Sellers in the film version, is founded on an eternal rule: People hear what they want to hear, even if you are saying something completely different.

Many people lie every day, even if only in little ways. Somebody says "How're you doing?" and we usually say "fine" even if we feel lousy. Do otherwise and you've violated a social bargain to lie, because the truth is not what people really want to hear. Blessed are those who really are interested when they ask how you are doing, but, sadly, they are not common.

Of course, our lying is often more calculated. Abraham Lincoln was a good liar. When running for the U.S. Senate, he managed to portray himself as being both for and against slavery, depending on who was listening.

To audiences of antislavery voters in his famous debates with Stephen Douglas, he talked of the wrongs of slavery. But for proslavery voters Lincoln made it seem as though he endorsed prejudiced claims that blacks were inferior, saying he saw no "equality between the white and the black races."

Despite his verbal gymnastics in the Lincoln-Douglas debates, Old Abe lost that campaign, but for long afterward he sought the political expediency of having it both ways on racial issues. Even when freeing the slaves with the Emancipation Proclamation, Lincoln applied it to only the Confederate states, taking care not to upset the handful of slaveholding states in the Union.

Machiavelli would have greatly admired Lincoln's finesse on such a politically tricky issue. Successful politicians make effective use of our need to hear what we want to hear. They parse their words in a way that sounds better to our ears than how the literal text might look to our eyes.

## The Difference between What You Mean and How You Say It

In his first presidential campaign, Bill Clinton promised not to "raise taxes to pay for his programs." The statement was widely hailed as a promise against all tax increases. But Clinton did not emphasize that he only promised not to raise taxes *to pay for new programs*. In the literal text, he kept open the option to raise taxes on existing programs, which is what he ended up doing in office. By some calculations Clinton raised taxes more than any president before him, despite the appearance of his campaign promises to the contrary.

This is the Machiavellian way. If your actual words mean something different than how you are interpreted, you have laid a record that protects you from a charge of outright lying, and for the moment you have given the listeners what they wanted. Machiavelli said, "Men are so simple and yield so readily to the desires of the moment that he who will trick will always find another who will suffer to be tricked." Circus maestro P. T. Barnum updated Machiavelli's sixteenth-century prose with the famous line "There is a sucker born every minute."

Simply because it is easy does not always make it good politics to play this game. What happens when the lie is discovered? Here is where the masters are separated from the amateurs. The skilled liar responds to challenges by reverting to the literal text and the protection that it was originally meant to provide, even though it might contradict the impressions originally communicated.

Express outrage that anyone could have misinterpreted you, even though that is exactly what you had expected and wanted to happen. Your listener might not buy it entirely, but if done well, it creates enough confusion to get you off the hook. It worked for Clinton.

## LYING FOR A GOOD CAUSE

Many times people cannot or will not "handle the truth," as Jack Nicholson's military character asserted in the film *A Few Good Men*. Families often face situations where they think it best not to tell a loved one really bad news. Or they encourage loved ones with lies. When a child learns to cook, parents pretend to enjoy it.

People used to call such fabrications a "white lie," even teaching their children that it is just fine to make up stuff if it really doesn't matter or if it is for a good purpose. This must really confuse the children, who also hear over and over again about the evils of lying.

The existence of Santa Claus is one of our society's grandest lies. We nurture children to believe in a lie for fun. Once they figure out that no one flies around the world distributing gifts to every kid on Earth in a single night, they have learned a strange lesson about our culture's seemingly hypocritical indulgence in the joy and reality of lying.

As Mark Twain said, "Truth is a precious thing, which is why we use it sparingly."

It is not a long philosophical journey from lying to produce better-behaved children—the underlying purpose of the Santa Claus ritual—to lying to manipulate anyone else for any other good purpose. And once this sort of lying is considered acceptable, the door is open to abuse.

Whether for good or evil, lying is an oft-deployed tool in the manipulation of others. Success depends on how convincingly the lie is delivered. Most people possess intuitive and remarkably accurate lie detectors that, if only in the subconscious, tip them off when they are being fed a lie. These detectors mostly depend on physical and verbal clues such as a nervous tone of voice, shifty eyes, and uneven body movements.

Bad liars are better off telling the truth or saying nothing at all. A friend of mine is the worst liar that I have ever known. Even if he tries to say something innocuous or routinely complimentary, he cannot do it convincingly if he does not believe it. He cannot even manage to sound interested in the weather, as so many of us pretend to do when we desperately need to make small talk. Realizing this deficiency, he often chooses to remain quiet at the times when most people spout fraudulent inanities to sound pleasant. And he accepts the usual consequence that the liar in the room ends up being the most popular.

While most people can pull off the tiny lies to meet social conventions, only a few expert liars are able to train their bodies to conceal the telltale signs of a whopping lie. Some even manage to deceive scientific instruments designed to detect lies.

For the amateur liar, there is another way: Convince yourself of the truthfulness of your lie. Your body might respond appropriately if your brain is not fully aware of the lie, thus failing to trigger physical ticks that reveal your lying ways. Of course, this too requires considerable discipline and perhaps a dash of self-delusion.

I see this phenomenon quite often as a journalist covering politicians in Washington, D.C. Some can be handed a set of talking points that present one bald-faced lie after another, but they actually seem to convince themselves that they are telling the truth. And the results are remarkable. Not everyone believes them, but if there are enough people out there who desperately want to believe the same untruths, the politician most certainly gets away with it.

Determined liars are well advised to develop an alternative, but somewhat truthful, version of their words, as a technique for convincing themselves that they are not lying. This is probably how Bill Clinton was able to fool so many for so long when he claimed that he did not have sexual relations with his White House intern Monica Lewinsky. Since the two did not have intercourse, which is how Clinton chose to define "sexual relations," he was able to passionately assert his denial.

## Truth Tellers Get Caught

Oscar Wilde said that he had intended to create only a "pleasing paradox" when he wrote that those who tell the truth will be "found out." And as the paradox he meant it to be, the line certainly seems self-contradictory while ringing a bit true.

There is so much lying in the world, especially in politics, that telling the truth can easily shock people to the point of being almost scandalous. Indeed, one should be more careful about telling the truth than about telling a lie. If the truth is unpopular, it is probably best kept to yourself. If the lie is what people want to hear, you can go ahead and tell it, but be sure that you have a backup plan in case your lie becomes unpopular.

# Ambition Is Never Satisfied

*The ass went seeking for horns and lost his ears.*
ARABIAN PROVERB

Without ambition, we would still be living in caves. Ambition separates humans from animals. Humans strive, while animals endure. Ambition can be dangerous. Adolph Hitler was ambitious. But so was Gandhi.

Choosing your ambition is the first step. We nag children with the question "What do you want to be when you grow up?" It is a question that we should never stop asking of ourselves. Many adults go through life without an answer.

Whatever ambition we choose, no matter how modest, we use politics to get there. Even if you simply aspire to be well liked, you will have to play politics to persuade others to like you. If you want to be a good parent, you must learn to manipulate your children to make you proud and have others praise your parenting skills.

Ambition is dangerous in the hands of those with evil goals. But that is not its only danger. It consumes those in its grip.

Machiavelli: "Ambition is so powerful a passion in the human breast, that however high we reach we are never satisfied."

Indeed, ambition is like a drug, a healing force also capable of doing great harm to its addicts.

Corporations are driven by the principle of never-ending ambition to profit. In capitalist economies, profits must grow, or the company falters. The ambition is never satisfied. More profits only create an expectation for more and more to come.

In the early twenty-first century, the energy company Enron was run by ruthlessly ambitious executives. They found numerous ways to falsify and inflate profits, to the point that the company collapsed when their criminal methods were discovered. Employees and investors lost everything.


### Even the Microwave Is Too Slow

There is a touch of Enron greed in everyone. Our standard of living might be lower than where we want to be. Our house is not big enough. Our gadgets are not advanced enough. Our airlines are not fast enough. Some even get impatient waiting for the microwave to heat a plate of food. The loftier our ambitions, the more insatiable they become, devouring less-demanding ambitions.

Aim too high and you leave no room for simpler and possibly more pleasing ambitions, such as meaningful relationships, personal growth, and good parenting. The young lawyer loses a marriage to obsessing with work. A corporate success story is hated by his children. The rich man has no real friends.

Those who reach the top of the charts—presidents, Olympic champions, Nobel scientists—usually get there by making their ambition rule their lives. Once achieving such heights, ambitious superstars cannot get enough. Once elected, the president struggles for reelection and a legacy that leads to a prominent place in history books. Olympic athletes chase medals until their bodies will not allow them to go on. Those governed by power and wealth never stop trying to accumulate it.

## Define Your Limits

It is vital to define the limits of your ambition, or risk never being satisfied. As a child, I wanted to grow up to be president of the United States. I was seized by this ambition through my late teens and barely into my late twenties. It threatened to govern the rest of my life and drive me insane—until I had an epiphany. One day a very angry man on his front lawn showered me with his water sprinkler and changed my life.

I was running for the state legislature at the age of twenty-six, fulfilling my long-held ambition to get elected to something and one day become president. That summer and fall I knocked on at least three thousand doors, hustling myself to the district's neighborhoods.

That is when I encountered the bitterly angry man who had some sort of beef against politicians in general. He told me to get lost, picked up a running sprinkler, and pointed it at me. Luckily, it was a hot day in Florida, and the water felt pretty good.

The incident preyed on me, but its full significance did not hit home until the day after I lost the election. All the pain and suffering of that campaign—symbolized by getting doused with a sprinkler—probably felt stronger because I had lost. But I suddenly felt relieved and somehow realized that losing was the best thing that could have happened to me. I was free of this ambition. I no longer wanted to be president of the United States.

I still loved politics and eventually found my way into journalism as an outlet. Now I cover presidents for a living, which turned out to be the right fit for my childhood ambition. Watching presidents come and go—and observing the hundreds of politicians in Washington making themselves miserable trying to become president—I now think that the job of president is a lousy job, not worth the torture of seeking, and I thank God that I learned at an early age to abort that ambition.

But my early desires and that singular experience as a candidate for office give me empathy for politicians. One must crave public adoration with such intensity that not even setbacks such as getting hosed by a voter will dissuade one from running for office. In some ways I think that the best politicians are like the best trial lawyers, another occupation I toyed with for a while. In both cases, the most successful are those who will do anything to win the love of voters or jurors, desperate to avoid losing because they would see it as personal rejection.

In other words, the best politicians and trial lawyers are often the most insecure people in the room, needing acceptance so intensely that failure is not an option, or their own self-worth is called into question. And if they are lucky, they are blinded to these facts, driven only by the more tangible ambition to win office or win a trial. And if the intensely ambitious are successful in their pursuits, bless them all, for they have at least found happiness in this one arena of life, even if it comes at great cost.

Excessive ambition comes at another cost: loss of control. If you will do anything anyone asks of you to achieve a fantastic ambition, you have given up control. Better to be on the other side of the equation—the one harnessing and reaping the benefits of another's insatiable, potentially destructive ambition. You then have the control.

If someone at work is hysterically ambitious to win a promotion, you might form a bond with him or her and work together. Either you will rise as the other worker rises or the boss will decide that you have better sense, giving you the promotion.

Plenty marry ambitious people just for the material benefits that go with it. Others marry ambition to harness it. Hillary Clinton used her husband's ambition to win her own office.

So long as you are feeding ambitious people what they crave, you control them. Make their dreams come true and you own them.

This is why most companies seek ambitious workers— they jump through more hoops, willingly suffer indignities, and, above all, follow orders. Beware the boss who encourages you to buy a house or a new car. Mortgages and car payments enslave you to the paycheck that your boss controls.

## Careful What You Wish For

Western culture might gain something from the Arab proverb warning about the ass that lost his ears looking for his horns—or, put a different way, careful what you wish for. You might get it.

Societies that preach ambition get more done, make more money, and win more wars. But they tend to overdo it.

Americans, in particular, are examples of great success derived from unbridled ambition. We call it the American Dream, and it certainly provides a comfortable life for those who reach it.

It also makes us vulnerable to those who see a bigger picture. Look at how the Japanese decimated the U.S. automobile industry by doing a better job of understanding and supplying demand fueled by the insatiable American dream to own the coolest car on the block. Funny how the Japanese knew better than to create such a voracious car culture in their own country, instead focusing on mass transportation that so many smog-filled American cities never got done.

Better to limit your own ambition and harness the ambition of those who have no control over theirs. You will be in charge.

## Only the Flexible Succeed

*Eighty percent of success is showing up.*
WOODY ALLEN

$S$tanding tall looks good in a John Wayne movie, but as the song goes, "You gotta know when to fold 'em." Great leaders are more flexible than they appear. The trick is to bend without anyone noticing. Machiavelli: "Whosoever desires constant success must change his conduct with the times."

Cher did it. The American entertainer is a model of flexible career management. A chart-topping singer, television star, Academy Award winner, rock 'n' roller, disco diva, and fashion icon, Cher reinvented herself over and over again during nearly five decades on the national stage.

"I've always taken risks," Cher told an interviewer in 2002. "I never worried what the world might really think of me."

Convincingly portraying oneself as immune to the opinions of others, as Cher does in the aforementioned quote, is the key to success for those who are truly skilled in the art of doing quite the opposite. While Cher ably cultivated the image of a rebel who does not care what others think, her many and varied career victories were actually based on constantly reshaping her image according to what people think. In Cher's case, she studiously followed the evolving demands of the cultural marketplace, billing each dramatic turnaround of style as another example of rebellion—an image that allowed her to make calculated changes while appearing to be consistent.

Above all, flexible winners must not let others see them sweat, making strategic adjustments that seem to follow a natural course. People might say that they admire consistency, but in truth they reward the flexible.

Many times throughout her career Cher found success by changing "with the times," as Machiavelli prescribed. When her marriage to singing partner Sonny Bono broke up in the mid-1970s, she made it on her own as a solo performer, skillfully shifting musical styles through the years, from easy-listening pop to edgy rock rhythms to hard-pounding disco. When her album sales slowed to a crawl in the early 1980s, Cher turned herself into a serious film actor and won an Oscar. The movie success renewed interest in her music and at age forty-one in 1987, Cher was back on the charts as a top singer, staying there for two more decades and culminating with a 2008 Las Vegas show deal reportedly paying $60 million—to a woman already considered to be one of the wealthiest players in the entertainment industry.

## Einstein's Definition of Insanity

Lucky for most of us we do not have to tailor our lives and ambitions to the frenzied whims of music consumers. But even if it is to a lesser degree, the flexibility required to reach our goals is worth thinking about. Openness to change is a hallmark of success in any venue.

Even driving down the highway is an exercise in flexibility. Wouldn't it be wonderful if we could just set the cruise control and maintain a certain speed for a long drive? But neither life nor the highways work that way. When you hit a stretch of open highway devoid of competing drivers, you can cruise at any stable rate of your choosing.

But we are not alone. There are others around us traveling at varying speeds, moving in different directions, and presenting numerous obstacles to be maneuvered around. Rigidly keep the cruise control of life set to a single speed, and sooner or later you will crash into something or someone.

Still, it is important to keep in mind that people most respect leaders who seem confident and firm in the course that they have chosen. "Stay the course" is a popular slogan for U.S. presidents seeking reelection. Never mind that in most cases those who win second terms do so by making many adjustments in course.

Even George W. Bush, who built a winning image as a man of steadfast principles and unyielding direction, was far more flexible than he ever let on. In pursuing a war in Iraq, he persistently portrayed himself as sticking to a single course, unmoved by growing criticism.

Never mind that the Bush administration's course in Iraq changed many times. While claiming constancy, the president's war team veered in all directions, from chasing the illusion of massively destructive weapons to the on-again, off-again attitude toward seeking the help of experienced Iraqi military personnel. Add to that the unrealized predictions of thankful Iraqis greeting U.S. troops as liberators—and the initial failure of having an American civilian, L. Paul Bremer, run things—and you have a policy that never stayed on any particular course.

"Stay the course" works as a slogan for many situations, and people should maintain the image of constancy while adjusting their path behind the scenes whenever necessary.

Never stay on a course that is not working. After all, the main characters in the 1991 film *Thelma and Louise* stayed the course—and subsequently sailed off a cliff to their presumed death.

Refusing to alter your course when headed for certain doom recalls Albert Einstein's immortal definition of insanity: Doing the same thing over and over again and expecting different results.

## PLAY TO YOUR STRENGTHS, BUT DO NOT OVERLOOK YOUR WEAKNESSES

In the sixth century BC, the writer Sun Tzu produced *The Art of War*, a text still on the reading list at modern military schools. He wrote that "a wise general considers both the advantages and disadvantages opened to him." When considering the advantages, "he makes his plan feasible; when considering the disadvantages, he finds ways to extricate himself from the difficulties."

Many people fail to succeed in a situation because they do not fully consider their own weaknesses. Clearly seeing disadvantage, on the battlefield or in daily life, is vital to a winning strategy. Pretending that obstacles do not exist can guarantee failure.

To some, acknowledging a weakness is believed to be a weakness itself. Not so. Sure, you do not need to go around broadcasting your problems to others. Indeed, it is probably better to keep it to yourself. But it is critically important that you do not live in denial. Strength begins with being fully aware of your weakness. How can you play to your strengths if you cannot see what puts you at a disadvantage?

A football team with a quarterback who cannot reliably throw a completed pass should instead focus on its running game. I played for such a team once. Our quarterback could not see that his throwing arm was our weakest link, resisting our coach's efforts to develop his skill at handing off to strong running backs. We lost a lot of games.

Extricating yourself from difficulties, as Sun Tzu noted, is a key to success. Avoid putting yourself in a position of weakness. If you know that you might be ill-equipped for a particular task, do not volunteer for it. Find something else that plays to your strength.

Still, there are times when you must leverage victory from a position of weakness. Plainly acknowledging your situation, at least to yourself, will go a long way toward getting around it.

Being confident and acknowledging weaknesses are not mutually exclusive. Be confident about your strengths. Knowing where you are not strong allows you to improve in those areas. Ignoring weakness prevents progress.

Remaining flexible in the face of disadvantage will help you navigate around your obstacles. Develop alternate strategies for those areas where you are at a disadvantage. There is nothing worse than discovering a weakness when it is too late to overcome it.

## Start a Big Job by Doing One Thing

Woody Allen did a bit more than just show up to succeed in his filmmaking career, but he was not off base in observing that getting ahead depends on showing up. Approach any task ready to play. Whining about the obstacles, or pretending there are none, is not showing up.

For any important project, you need a strategy. So many people blunder into situations ill-prepared or overconfident about their abilities. They usually fail or barely get by.

Sometimes a job just seems too insurmountable, and you cannot get yourself fired up to even show up in the first place. I came across some good advice when I was just beginning to write this book. My editor said, "Just do one thing today."

That simple line got me started. At the beginning, I did at least one thing every day, no matter how little it was. Every small step forward meant that I was gaining ground. Before long, I was doing many things a day, enough so that the day finally came when the book was finished.

There are always obstacles to progress. Be aware of them, but do not be ruled by them. Keeping your options open in the face of difficulty will help you steer your way to success.

Rigidity is your enemy. The inflexible only go so far. They might be content with their standing in life, but they have most likely missed opportunity—simply because they were not looking for it.

# Better to Imitate a Winner
# Than Be an Original Loser

*A good imitation is the most perfect originality.*
VOLTAIRE

Coal miners once lowered canaries down shafts to test the air. If the canary died, they did not go in. Wise politicians avoid playing canary in the coal mine, instead letting others take risks until the winning way is found.

Machiavelli: "A prudent man should always follow in the footsteps of great men and imitate those who have been outstanding. If his own prowess fails to compare with theirs, at least it has an air of greatness about it."

Advertisers follow a version of this rule. They know how to imitate success. Clairol won kudos in 1994 for a shockingly amusing commercial pitching Herbal Essence shampoo and featuring women shrieking with pleasure in the shower while using the product. The Clairol ad was patterned after a famous scene from the 1989 movie *When Harry Met Sally*, in which actress Meg Ryan convincingly mocks an orgasm in a crowded restaurant. The television commercial led to more copycat ads alluding to women's sexual satisfaction.

Meg Ryan was the canary who more than survived in pushing the limits of mainstream audience receptivity to a woman exhibiting such blatant sexuality. Largely on the strength of that one scene, the romantic comedy became her first full-blown hit. But Ryan also discovered the dangers of being original. The role typecast her as the feisty, bubbly ingénue, and she long struggled to take on more serious parts. Sometimes if your originality grows too popular, you can't be anything else. On the rare occasions when people bond with something new and different, they tend to insist that you repeat yourself and resist attempts to be original again.

Just about any shampoo bottle, not just Clairol's, carries the message of this rule: "Repeat often."

While an original success is considered a wonderful thing and widely praised, the odds favor a copy offering the better guarantee of success. Familiarity comforts people. The unrecognizable is discomforting.

## NEW INFORMATION SCARES PEOPLE

In my early days in journalism, a streetwise editor once told me that sometimes what we see as a strength of our profession—telling people what they don't know—could also be our downfall. In truth, this editor feared that "information scares people."

Newspaper editors and television news producers, like moviemakers and songwriters, struggle against the need among most consumers to be given stories that fit into patterns and formulas that they understand and recognize. I once saw this phenomenon in action with the local news coverage of a stabbing in Washington, D.C. A man was killed while visiting the home of friends. The police detectives released few details at first, but they did say that there was no sign of intrusion and that they believed that the victim had been targeted.

Local television news stations ignored the intriguing details suggesting that this was a truly mysterious story and instead focused on the threat of home invasions, interviewing random citizens on the street about their fear of burglaries. Clearly, putting this crime into a recognizable category made it easier to report and consume, even though the facts of the case pointed to something quite different.

There are lessons for everyday life in the imitative tactics of successful advertisers, entertainment executives, and news professionals. Be very cautious about choosing when to present an idea or a behavior that people are not expecting. Be too original too often and you might please yourself, but others might turn away.

The workplace is a dangerous venue for originality. Most of your coworkers will probably resist something as minor as a new idea for where to eat lunch. Try to suggest entirely new ways of doing their work and you could quickly become the most unpopular person in the office, no matter how brilliant your ideas might be.

People do not like change. And originality brings change to their lives. Better to fit your ideas into the context of what they recognize—better yet to give them ownership of your new ideas—because people do like to think of themselves as being original, even if they do not reward it in others. This is particularly true of most bosses. If you want something from them, you are more likely to get it if you patiently take the time to make it their idea. If you want a new assignment or even a promotion, do not immediately ask for it without carefully laying a foundation. Instead, be subtle about it. Find ways to show them that you can do whatever it is you are wanting to do, and see if the idea of their formally giving it to you naturally occurs to them. In many cases you might eventually have to ask, but the payoff of not having to ask is worth the extra time for groundwork.

For better results, connect your original ideas to something others want or to something familiar and pleasant. Children learn crude versions of this trick quite early in life. "Buy me a new computer because it will make me a better student," they beg. Of course, they might really want it to play the latest video games.

## How to Catch an Idea Thief

You finally have an original idea, and someone steals it. What then? You know the type. They are human sponges, soaking up the words and thoughts of others, never giving credit once they have absorbed your intellectual property and made it their own. Sometimes these human sponges do not even realize that they have stolen an idea. It is just an intuitive process outside the realm of their own consciousness. That can be even more infuriating, to hear someone repeat something that you have said and then not even remember where it came from.

I have never found a mature-sounding way to say, "Hey, I said that first." It always comes out sounding like a little kid jealously protecting his toys. And after all, we cannot go around copyrighting all that we say or think. That would be cumbersome, indeed.

There is probably little we can do about the innocent thief who genuinely does not remember that you deserve credit or that anyone else ever said something first. They really think that it originated with them. This is the only way that unoriginal people have to live the lie that they are nothing but copycats.

The intentional thief is another matter. Identifying one can be tough. Most likely, if confronted, intentional thieves will pretend to be innocent, making you look prickly and immature. You need to take action once you suspect that a malicious idea thief is on the loose, usually because they have stolen from you a few times and have taken the credit that you deserved to their own advantage.

Start by catching them in the act. If they are knowingly stealing, then they are probably taking care not to claim credit in your presence. Here is where you might have the upper hand. Do not tip them off that you are onto their scam. You want them to keep at it until you have nailed them.

Consider to whom they might be passing along their little fraud. In the workplace, the boss is an obvious one. Outside your presence, they might be currying favor with your ideas. You might want to make up something for them to pass on that you will likely hear repeated back to you by the person they are talking to. You will have your proof.

If you really want to be devious, come up with something that you know that the boss does not like or does not want to hear. Plant this item with your suspect and keep watch. If the culprit is as guilty as you think, the ruse could backfire on him—and your victory will be sweet.

## When in Doubt, Imitate—but Do It Well

If you are going to imitate others—and it often pays to do so—then be good at it. Above all, you do not want to get caught. Make your imitation as good as the original but different in enough ways that you will not be found out.

Voltaire was not being trite in noting that a good imitation can be as perfect as the original. Indeed, it should be. It might even be better than the original. Imitations of great art works often look better than the originals.

If you lack the creativity to take someone else's ideas and rework them as your own, then perhaps you had better not try. Imitation done well is not plagiarism, which is wholesale copying without any changes made or credit given. I have taken care not to plagiarize Machiavelli in this book but instead use his words as a starting place for my own journey. I have taken his advice to heart, following in the footsteps of a great man, which, if nothing else, has an "air of greatness about it."

Building your own world on the foundation of others is an admirable contribution. Thinking that you should only do or say things that are completely original is unrealistic in most cases, and you might not get very much done. Be not afraid. Be an original imitator.

# Never Keep Your Word
# If Circumstances Change

*It is true you may fool all the people some of the time;*
*you can even fool some of the people all the time;*
*but you can't fool all of the people all of the time.*
ABRAHAM LINCOLN

It is a staple of "gotcha" jour-
nalism, catching politicians breaking their word but refusing
to admit it. It is great sport among civilians, too. Failing to
keep track of promises—yours and those of others—can get
you into trouble. Shifting stance without getting caught is
one of the most difficult strokes in the art of politics.

"A prudent ruler cannot, and must not, honor his word
when it places him at a disadvantage and when the reasons
for which he made his promise no longer exist," Machiavelli
wrote.

Whether holding great power or protecting yourself
against those who have it, be careful to understand the nature of making promises and never consider them etched in
stone. A promise can be illusory, because to make a promise,
one must predict the future. On the most rudimentary level,
you make a promise when you schedule a doctor's appoint-
ment, saying that you will be there at some future date and

time. But when the day arrives, what if circumstances prevent your being there as scheduled? You have broken your promise.

Because promises always depend on the cooperation of circumstances that one cannot predict, they are more often broken than kept. And the powerful find it much easier than the less powerful to go back on their word, because they have the clout to make others accept it.

Catching politicians breaking promises or contradicting their past words is a favorite pastime for the news media. Rarely do the accused ever say, "Yeah, I changed my mind." Usually, they struggle to make changing positions appear consistent, with varying degrees of skill and success. Those who are good at shifting positions seamlessly tend to survive better than those who too freely admit their inconsistencies.

Senator John Kerry of Massachusetts is a case study in how not to characterize your flexibility. While campaigning as the 2004 Democratic presidential nominee, he talked about the apparent contradiction in his votes on Iraq war legislation, saying that he voted for it before he voted against it. That earned him the spotlight in opposing television commercials, adding to his reputation as a flip-flopper.

When your changing positions are so obvious and numerous that people notice, your skill set in this area needs some work. But you also do not want to be inflexible or brag too much about being someone who never goes back on your word. This just alerts others to monitor your words until they find something inconsistent, no matter how minor it might be.

Perhaps the biggest mistake of Jimmy Carter's political life was his 1976 presidential campaign promise that he would "never lie." Although it helped him win the White House in the wake of the corruption of the Watergate years, Carter's vow put him in a political straitjacket.

Applying such an inflexible standard of truth telling to himself made Carter vulnerable to charges of hypocrisy whenever political expediency demanded that he shade the truth. And he found little advantage when he held true to his promise. He earned a reputation for painful honesty on subjects ranging from his obsession with the dangers of dependency on foreign oil to ending U.S. support of foreign dictators in Iran and Nicaragua.

But instead of the accolades that he hoped to gain by telling the truth on subjects that earlier presidents dodged, Carter became a laughingstock to cynical media elites and political power players in Washington. That derision eventually spread around the country, giving Ronald Reagan ample fodder to defeat Carter for reelection in 1980.

## CANDOR LOOKS BETTER IN HINDSIGHT

In later years, Carter's candor and moral compass made him one of the most popular ex-presidents in history. But if by some happenstance Carter returned to the presidency after restoring his popularity, the honesty so admired in his private life would again defeat him in office.

In any situation, you cannot hold power by always telling the truth. If you are determined to be a scrupulously honest person, then, like Carter, you had better be prepared to live a life without much power. And you should be exceedingly skeptical of believing the word of anyone who holds great power over you.

It is tempting to believe the powerful. The rich person who shows interest in you has the power to make you rich. A powerful boss could give you an enticing promotion. But always guard yourself with the knowledge that few among the rich and powerful got there by always keeping their word. If circumstances change and their promises to you no longer benefit them as they once did, you will be forgotten.

It is good policy to appear to trust the powerful, as they generally want to be considered people of integrity; but in plotting your course, keep in mind a contingency plan for the possibility that you might one day be of no use to them.

Most employees of the Enron company deeply believed in the power and wealth of their bosses until the energy firm went bankrupt in 2001. Workers poured their life savings into the company, lured by promises of fabulous wealth. But even as those executives were urging employees to invest, they were storing money elsewhere because, as it turned out, they were lying all along about Enron's financial health.

Not every powerful person whom you encounter will be as slimy and corrupt as an Enron convict, but better to be skeptical than broke.

## How to Break a Promise

Be on guard against those who are setting you up for a broken promise. The clever ones take great pains to make you see how unreasonable it is to keep their promise.

Bill Clinton had to break a promise to the people of Arkansas when he decided to run for president in 1992. In his earlier campaign for reelection as the state's governor, he had to deal with suspicions that he planned a White House run. Opponents argued that Clinton was just using Arkansas as a staging ground, that he had no intention of finishing his term in the governor's mansion.

Promising that he would not run for president in 1992, Clinton persuaded the voters to keep him in office as governor. But then circumstances changed. Fewer strong Democrats than expected entered the presidential race to challenge incumbent George Herbert Walker Bush. Clinton had an opening to run that he had not expected when he made his promise to the people of Arkansas.

Clinton wisely did not just ignore his promise. He toured the state arguing his case for why Arkansas could greatly benefit if he won the White House race. What could have become a national issue damaging Clinton's credibility to voters outside Arkansas never really gained traction against him, because he had so convincingly persuaded most in his home state to forgive his broken promise.

Of course, any savvy person might have known that his initial promise meant little if it turned out the ambitious Clinton got the opportunity to run for office while his promise against it was in effect.

Be wary of promises that do not seem likely to be kept and do not take into account the probability that circumstances will change. Likewise, if you are faced with the need to break a promise, consider Clinton's lesson. It might be tempting to pretend that you never made the promise, but this infuriates people, earning you lasting enemies. The better course is the one that Clinton pursued.

Acknowledge that you made a promise that now must be broken. Apologize profusely. You might still generate anger, but the odds are lower than if you lie about ever having made the promise in the first place.

Make a strong case for how the changing circumstances causing you to break your word were unforeseeable when you made the promise. And most important, if at all possible, develop convincing reasons for why breaking the promise actually benefits those to whom you had made it.

## Playing the Fool

Fooling all of the people all of the time is not easy, but it is not impossible, as Abraham Lincoln claimed in his famous quote. Maybe he should have said that you cannot fool all of the people *forever*, which is probably what he meant. Even those who get away with it are found out someday, but the truth does not often emerge until after they are long dead.

I have seen plenty of clever types fool everyone all of the time and get away with it, even when they are found out. They just fool everyone again with disingenuous apologies for fooling them the first time.

Still, Lincoln's advice is practical. Yes, you can get away with plenty in this world. People should not be as gullible as they are, assuming that someone's word is his or her bond. No matter how many times they are fooled, some people belly right back up to the bar for another round of getting fooled.

But living a life of getting your way with broken promises and fraudulent claims is bound to catch up with you. Living a life assuming that you cannot be fooled will catch up with you, too. Remember what could be considered a corollary to Lincoln's rule: Fool me once, shame on you. Fool me twice, shame on me.

## To Control Others,
## First Walk in Their Shoes

*If you would become a master of men,*
*you must become a servant of men.*
BENJAMIN DISRAELI

In *Aesop's Fables*, the North Wind and the Sun argue about which is the more powerful, so they agree on a plan to settle the dispute. The victor will be the one who can strip a wayfaring man of his clothes.

The North Wind went first, summoning his power and blowing gusts of wind with all of his might. But the keener his blasts, the closer the traveler wrapped his cloak around him. Giving up hope, the Wind called upon the Sun to see what he could do.

The Sun shone out all of his warmth. The traveler, sweltering from the intense rays, began removing one garment after another and, at last, nearly overcome with heat, undressed and bathed in a nearby stream.

The lesson of the Sun's victory: Persuasion is better than force. To persuade others, we must know them. Understanding their needs, motivations, and intentions makes it easier to provide the right mix of tools to persuade them to do what you want them to do.

If you have sufficient power over someone, you could simply order them to do your bidding. But even then, you are likely to get better results if you find a way to make the task something that he or she wants to do. Sure, it is more work for you to spend time figuring these things out, but keeping people happy is the best way to get them to do their best.

Being a student of other people comes in handy in many other ways, large and small. Even if you are just trying to stay out of someone's way, you will find better success if you learn where they are going. Walking across a busy street is much safer if you take care to determine the intentions of oncoming drivers. Even if you have the legal right-of-way, you never know when a moving vehicle might run the red light and run you down. Better to make eye contact with any drivers coming your way. This ensures that they see you, and it helps you make a determination whether you are on a collision course with them.

## Keep Your Guard Up with a Smile

Life is like walking along a crowded street no matter what the circumstances. In the office, at school, even sitting around the family dinner table, always taking stock of what other people are up to will help you make your own way with greater ease.

Understanding human nature is your starting point, whether seeking to manipulate others or guarding against being manipulated. It is no surprise that Machiavelli's view of human nature was supremely cynical. "Of mankind we may say in general they are fickle, hypocritical, and greedy of gain," he said.

Even if Machiavelli's conclusion is overly harsh, it is best to keep it in mind as your default view until proven otherwise. Fickle, hypocritical, and greedy describe many people. Assuming that a stranger fits one or all of these categories helps you avoid mistakes in dealing with them. But be quick to adjust if they exhibit a better nature, or risk forcing them into less admirable behavior.

Curiosity is your most effective tool in evaluating another. Ask questions. People like to talk about themselves. Try this experiment. Get into a conversation with someone and only ask questions. Make them simple, easy-to-answer, nonthreatening questions: What did you do last night? Where were you born?

Let the other person talk as much as he likes. Just listen. If there is a pause, ask another question that naturally flows from what he has just said. Resist any temptation to embark on your own commentary. You will not learn anything about someone else if you do all of the talking.

Expect two positive results from this experiment. The other person will likely walk away thinking that you are a great conversationalist and will probably not even realize that you said very little. Many people try too hard to make too many of their own points in a conversation, thinking that is the way to impress people. Not true. As a rule, most prefer the sound of their own voices to yours.

Second, and most important, prodding others to talk about themselves is how you learn necessary information for analyzing their needs, motivations, and intentions. The more you know about them and the less they know about you, the better you will be able to control them—or avoid being controlled.

This process does not have to be about cynically manipulating people like pawns on a chessboard, although that certainly was Machiavelli's purpose in writing about the techniques of power. Being interested in others, exhibiting genuine curiosity about their lives, creates a happy workplace, a pleasing home life, and can even produce more positive interactions with strangers.

My grandfather was a master at the art of praising restaurant waiters and others, too. We always got better service when dining with him. That was not his purpose. He was genuinely interested in people and always empathized with restaurant workers because he ran a restaurant himself for many years. But at a young age, I observed how effective his pleasant manner could be. He was quick to notice someone with a smile, no matter how fleeting it was. "What a pleasant smile," he would say. Sometimes, that was all that it would take to persuade someone to do anything that he wanted, giving him special attention and having a wonderful time doing it.

## THE POWER OF SILENCE

What do you do when there is a lull in the conversation? If you are like me and many others, your tendency is to fill the void with chatter. But sometimes it is better to embrace the silence. If you are in a negotiation or some other serious conversation, nervous chatter implies weakness or insecurity.

Some people use silence almost as a weapon, knowing that it makes others uncomfortable. Some people keep quiet because they do not have anything meaningful or intelligent to say. Either way, the effect is the same.

Even a stupid person can give the appearance of being in charge by saying nothing while someone else prattles on. Abraham Lincoln said, "Better to remain silent and thought a fool, than to speak up and remove all doubt." But the odds are that remaining silent at times will not risk one's being thought a fool.

I had a boss once who used silence effectively. He would just listen. I noticed that he learned a lot this way. People are less guarded when they are desperately trying to fill the silence. They pass on gossip or reveal things that they might not have said if the other person were keeping up the pace of the conversation.

It might seem rude to make someone else do all of the talking. Conversation should be like tossing a ball back and forth. If one person doesn't bother to catch the ball or throw it back, nobody is having much fun. But this might be a useful technique when you need to dominate another person and you do not have anything to say that will do the job.

People imagine so much on their own in the face of silence. On the television game show *Wheel of Fortune*, Vanna White became a national sensation without ever uttering a word. She just looked pretty and turned the letters on the stage. But when she tried to break out of that role and pursue a singing career, she lost her mystique. People were not as intrigued anymore. All that they might have imagined her to be in her silence was probably too different from what she turned out to be when she started talking and singing. She never regained the prominence that she had enjoyed as a silent mystery. The Vanna White syndrome plays out often in life. Keeping quiet and letting others imagine what they like can be a powerful tool.

At the West Virginia cabin where I am working on this book, every afternoon a hungry gopher wanders by, rustling in the brush for food. The first day, the gopher stopped and looked at me. I started talking, and he immediately scurried away. The next day, I remained completely still and quiet. We maintained eye contact for several minutes, and every afternoon we had our special moment.

Letting the stillness happen in relations with human beings might also prove to be, for a moment anyway, more meaningful than filling the air with lots of empty words.

## MAKE SERVANTS OF THOSE YOU SERVE

Walt Disney World, in Orlando, where I was raised, fascinates me as a study in the brilliant manipulation of human behavior. The theme park attracts millions of visitors every year, applying former British prime minister Benjamin Disraeli's rule that you become a master of others by serving them well.

The Disney way is to cater to the visitors' every whim and then take all of their money. Flying home to Orlando one time, I sat next to a family en route to what was to be their eighth consecutive annual visit to Disney World. I asked the father why he and his family took all of their summer vacations there. "Because," he said in all seriousness, "you just give them all of your money and they take care of everything."

Who is the master and who is the servant in that arrangement? On the surface, it seems that Disney is serving the customer. But through the years, the company's commitment to service allowed it to raise prices and hotel room rates beyond anything that its founder, Walt Disney, had ever imagined. In the end, I argue, the one making all of the money is the true master.

# The More Visible Your Power, the More Its Limits Are Known

*The less you use it the more you have.*
ANDREW YOUNG

Capitol Hill separates law-makers into two types: showboats and workhorses. Showboats are those who call attention to their power, dashing to the cameras, offering public comment on whatever the topic of the day might be. They are often the ones with the least power. Workhorses tend to avoid the limelight, working the levers behind the scenes and downplaying talk of their influence. They are often the ones with the most power.

Speaking softly and carrying a big stick still works as a general proposition for any purpose in life. Still, it is best to strike a balance. Even workhorses flex their muscles now and then. Machiavelli advised, "One must therefore be a fox to recognize traps and a lion to frighten the wolves."

Dick Cheney is a classic workhorse. As vice president to George W. Bush, he well understands the benefits of mystery in playing the power game of Washington, D.C. He has been around long enough to see what happens to those whose influence becomes a public spectacle.

Once the war against terror unfolded, Vice President Cheney's whereabouts became famously described as an "undisclosed location." This was not only a device for his security handlers to protect him. It also served as a metaphor for his secretive ways.

Most vice presidents get few turns in the spotlight but not for lack of trying. Cheney purposely avoids it, provoking much speculation about the extent of his influence in the Bush administration. Imaginations have run wild about the nature of his power, probably encouraging a view that he has far more clout than he actually wields.

Tom DeLay exemplified the show horse but with a twist. He also had real power. As majority leader of the House of Representatives during most of the Bush years, the Texas Republican relished his reputation as "the hammer." He was so named for his ruthless methods in prodding GOP lawmakers to do his bidding.

But Delay's high profile serves as a warning against making your power too visible. You become a target. He ended up facing criminal charges and being ousted from his leadership position largely because he invited scrutiny by showing so much force. And his methods gained many enemies along the way, foes who were only too happy to jump on him once he was down.

## Keeping Your Powder Dry

It is not surprising, therefore, that Cheney outlasted DeLay. Both were fierce warriors and compatriots in the cause of furthering a conservative agenda in Washington. But their contrasting public styles gave Cheney the better job security.

Still, Cheney was not averse to the occasional public roar, frightening the wolves, as Machiavelli advised. On the campaign trail, he often served as Bush's hatchet man, delivering the GOP team's harshest lines attacking their Democratic foes—Al Gore in 2000 and John Kerry in 2004.

Cheney's very public displays of partisanship during those campaigns were all the more effective because he had so patiently kept his powder dry. His attacks generated maximum news coverage simply because he normally stays behind the scenes.

Power does tend to dissipate if not used. I once drove my car so little that the battery went dead. And like an automobile, power should be well maintained without overuse, but it also needs to be exercised now and then.

Even if you have power, it should be used sparingly over others. If you are too heavy-handed, you might just hurt yourself. Sure, it is tempting to get your way in all things large and small, if you have the ability to do so. But a hunter who blindly sprays the field of prey with shotgun pellets will soon run out of ammunition and possibly miss the target. Better to pick your shots one at a time, making sure that you hit something and conserve resources for the next hunt.

Remain wary of your own power even when others celebrate it. Human nature can be fickle in this regard, putting someone on a pedestal and tearing him or her down later. Those who stay on top usually take care to keep their exalted position in perspective, even if they worked hard to get there. It is fine to succeed by promoting yourself, but never, ever believe your own hype.

Few Hollywood film stars ever seem to learn this lesson. So many box-office sensations ultimately end up struggling on the dinner theater circuit. Whenever you think that you are on top for good, listen to the lyrics of "That's Life," preferably, Frank Sinatra's version: "You're riding high in April, shot down in May."

I have always admired Hollywood's supporting players more than I have the supernovas who burn out in a flash, never to be heard from again. Solid character actors such as Walter Brennan, Martin Landau, Olympia Dukakis, and Whoopi Goldberg have enjoyed long and profitable careers. While many of the marquee stars whom they worked under have eventually disappeared, they have always found work. And some of the great ones, like Robert Duvall and Tommy Lee Jones, became star attractions in later life.

We cannot all be megastars for our entire careers. In Hollywood, the Paul Newmans and Meryl Streeps are quite rare. For better odds on long-term job security and personal happiness, it is advisable to aim lower than the very top.

But if your aim is high, be aware of the risks and manage your power and prestige with great care. You will be a target for the jealous and an enemy of your competitors.

## Divine Power of the Earthly Kind

God is the ultimate invisible power. The absence of objective or scientific proof that God even exists actually enhances God's power over humankind. For centuries, imaginations have run wild about the extent and purpose of God's power and all without God's ever appearing on any stage anywhere.

Not everyone believes in God, but plenty do, enough so that God has no need to speak to mere mortals or offer any other tangible sign of existence to maintain billions of followers. Still, they pour into the void an endless and always evolving variety of interpretations, signs, images, and stories designed to make God an earthly reality.

Even many of those who say that they do not believe in God will say they do believe in a spiritual force of some kind. This belief in a formless neo-God is still rooted in the great power of the conventional God, for even some of the unbelievers are determined to believe in something similar, even if they are just worshipping nature.

The story of God is a potent reminder of the human capacity to vividly believe in what cannot be seen, heard, or touched. It might be true that invisible power is actually more tangible than visible power.

But even believers in invisible power yearn for physical manifestations of its existence. Unscrupulous evangelists prey on the human need for a "sign from God." Some claim to be faith healers who can cure the sick and the lame. Despite how ridiculous it might seem to most people, I do not rule out the possibility that the power of mind over body can be so intense that someone can trigger a healing process simply by believing so strongly that his or her faith in God will heal oneself. If so, the invisible power of God could be far greater than many think.

You do not have to go around playing God to learn the political lesson from this divine phenomenon, but as in most things, it does not hurt to be more God-like. Just remember God's invisibility when you are tempted to make a showy spectacle of your power. What works for God might work for you.

Maintain some mystery about your own clout. Let others wonder how much power you really have. Their imaginations will invariably fill in the blanks, just as they do with God.

Without centuries of followers, prophets, and preachers to spread the word, God might not be a figment of the human imagination today. As such, encourage associates to speak openly about your power, taking care never to explicitly confirm or deny their claims. The occasional demonstration of your authority to these associates might be required to enlist them in the cause of broadcasting tales of your power to others, but limit these displays to your inner circle. The Bible describes God actually giving orders to a precious few, empowering them as representatives to the flock—an effective management technique for any leader.

## Sometimes You Must Use Power, or Lose It

Andrew Young, the former mayor of Atlanta, wisely noted that overused power can disappear entirely. The use of power tends to reveal exactly how much—or how little—you actually possess. But it is also true that keeping your powder dry can leave you unarmed when you need it most. It is possible to conserve your power too much. Spend it or lose it, some say about a president's political clout.

The threat that unused power will dissipate is most true for those, like U.S. presidents, who face clearly defined timetables for the existence of their power. A newly elected president is guaranteed only four years in office and just one more term after that if reelected.

Some White House observers believe that if a president cannot get an agenda enacted within the first year or two, then it is unlikely to ever become law. A newly elected president emits a glow of great power thanks to the endorsement just conferred by the voters. But the bulb dims over time, until or if that president is chosen for a second term. And even then, a second termer soon becomes a lame duck, weakened by the fact that the U.S. Constitution forbids another term.

Those with official limits on their power, whether in the White House or at the local Kiwanis club, have only so long to make their presence felt. Better that they use their power quickly than wait until it is almost gone.

## Arrogance Makes an Easy Target

*Whom the gods would destroy,*
*they first make mad with power.*
CHARLES A. BEARD

As a sixteen-year-old in school, George Washington learned the "Rules of Civility & Decent Behaviour in Company and Conversation." He wrote out his own copy of the 110 maxims commonly taught during his day. One rule in particular must have come to mind as he fought the arrogant British monarchy and its pompous generals nearly three decades later in the Revolutionary War.

"Play not the Peacock," was rule no. 54 in Washington's classroom exercise. Like many others in the document, this rule advised students to avoid pretentiousness and self-importance.

Historians have long tried to understand how Washington and his ragtag band of revolutionaries won a war against the mightiest military machine of their day. One explanation given is that the British were simply blinded by their own arrogance. This made them vulnerable to a weaker force that was clever enough to gain the advantage by shunning conventional military formations on the battlefield, making effective use of the element of surprise and conducting indirect assaults that repeatedly put the British off guard.

What Washington and his military thinkers accomplished is what anyone hopes to do when confronting an arrogant foe: Exploit the self-defeating nature of a superior attitude.

As the British demonstrated in the eighteenth century, arrogance is a blinding fault. Be glad when you encounter conceited people standing in your way. You have already won half of the battle—and it will not take long to find and exploit their weaknesses.

First, it is best to feed their arrogance and therefore maintain the hidden advantage that you have over them. Those who think of themselves as brilliant, for instance, never tire of hearing someone confirm their self-image. They tend not to question their own judgment, overlooking possible flaws in their thinking, which lead to their making critical mistakes that give you the upper hand.

Carelessness and narrow-mindedness are the most damaging byproducts of arrogance. It stands to reason that if you think that you can do no wrong, then you are more likely to ignore a better way. And you are probably going to overlook people who might actually be your superiors in some regard, making it quite easy for them to beat you.

Bette Davis entertainingly played arrogance as a character flaw in the 1950s melodrama *All about Eve*. Never has a film so wittily dissected the nature of self-importance, and many critics have said that Davis's portrayal of a Broadway diva might have been her greatest performance. Her character is bested by an upstart actress who feeds her mentor's ego to such a point that Davis's character never sees it coming when the young starlet rises above her on the stage, having exploited the older, more famous character's visions of grandeur. Once Davis's character realizes what has happened and decides to retaliate at a party that she is throwing, we get one of Hollywood's most memorable lines: "Fasten your seat belts, it's going to be a bumpy night."

Beware the arrogant people who finally discover that they have been duped. That is not a pretty sight and one to be studiously avoided if possible.

## LESSONS OF SEPTEMBER 11

Since the September 11, 2001, attacks on the United States, I have sometimes thought that, before these terrorist assaults, Americans were much like Davis's character in *All about Eve*, smug in our comfort zone believing that we were invincible to such things. And when we got our wake-up call, the whole country seemed to go into shock.

The al Qaeda terrorists exploited what they saw as our arrogance, with sinister determination, producing a horrible tragedy, the most deadly attack on U.S. soil in its entire history. Had U.S. leaders not been so confident about the improbability of what happened, the country might have been better guarded. And yet, when planes were flown as bombs into the World Trade Center in New York City, a commonly heard response was "How could we have known?" Never mind that terrorists bombed the same building a decade earlier. Surely that might have been a clue.

Even after wising up to the real threat of terrorism, the U.S. response at times recalled the conceit of the British in colonial times, believing that its superior military might would defeat any foe. But again, terrorists found advantage within our country's own confidence. Years after the 2003 invasion of Iraq, American forces struggled against insurgents skilled at the unconventional and often insane tactics of warfare that were designed to even the score against a stronger foe.

As with many of the rules in this book, making a target out of someone else's arrogance can be used for evil or good. The means of political skill are the same no matter what the end might be. But the means never justify the end if your exclusive purpose is to kill innocents.

America's deadly lesson in terrorism should teach us the dangers of allowing so many around the world to think of us as arrogantly squatting on our great wealth and advantage, ironically presenting ourselves as the modern version of the British in 1776. Even with so much to be justifiably proud of, it only makes us more vulnerable.

## FIGHT ARROGANCE WITH ARROGANCE

Sometimes you fight arrogance with even more arrogance. I learned this lesson years ago as a customer of a hotel in Madrid, Spain. Upon check-in, I encountered a concierge who treated me as a peasant subject instead of a paying customer.

It all started with my question about local places to eat. At first, the concierge completely ignored me even though he was not otherwise occupied. After a second and a third attempt to ask my question, he finally barked out a list of restaurant names that meant nothing to me.

Walking away completely stunned by this jerk's behavior, I decided to make him my project. With my usual friendliness and without being a pest, I made a few other requests over the course of my stay, sometimes just making up questions that I did not really need answered. Each time, he gave me the cold shoulder and a supremely arrogant tone.

Realizing that I could never charm this guy into a better attitude, I hit on a new tactic. I marched right up to him and began ordering him around, doing my best to duplicate the superior tone of voice that he had been using on me. The effect was as stunning to me as my first encounter had been: I had turned the tables. He jumped to his feet and energetically complied with everything I asked. By the time that I checked out, he was the one coming up with ideas for things to do for me.

From then on, whenever I come across an arrogant jerk who will not positively respond to a pleasant manner, I briefly turn myself into that arrogant Spaniard. And almost without fail, the response is the same. But I do this only when really necessary because I do not enjoy this behavioral tactic at all. I prefer to walk away from the arrogant jerks of the world, but sometimes you do not have that choice.

To me, there are few people more infuriating than those who force us into an unpleasant manner to get something done. But they exist, and, when it really matters, we cannot let them have their way. You probably will not be able to change them, and seldom will you be able to "kill them with kindness," as the saying goes.

Arrogance is an attitude. And a person's attitude is about as unchangeable as the shape of his or her face. While I won a small victory in learning how to improve the manners of that concierge, I am sure that he was just as unpleasant to the next affable customer who made the mistake of not treating him the way that he treats others.

## The Higher They Climb, the Farther They Fall

It is tough not to think of Richard Nixon when pondering Charles Beard's admonition that the gods destroy power addicts. Here was a man with tremendous skill at governing, a master politician, and a creative diplomat. It is a marvel that anyone with Nixon's less-than-glamorous looks and bizarre-sounding voice could rise to the presidency in the modern media age.

Nixon's demise is a testimonial to the possibility and peril that await those who understand politics and the manipulation of power as well as he did. On the surface, Nixon was a textbook Machiavellian, following the great political writer's rules as if he had written them himself.

But if we look closer, we can see how Nixon failed to heed Machiavelli's many warnings about the dangers of arrogant power and the risks of making enemies unnecessarily. Too many who follow Machiavelli's teachings seem to overlook these warnings, even though they are spread throughout his texts.

Before dispatching his White House team to develop enemies lists and before trying to cover up a burglary of political opponents, enraging Congress and the media—and, eventually, most of the American public—Nixon might have benefited from a quick review of "The Need to Avoid Contempt and Hatred," a chapter in *The Prince*, which Machiavelli used in order to show how his imaginary prince must avoid giving ammunition to his foes.

"One of the most powerful safeguards a prince can have against conspiracies is to avoid being hated by the populace," Machiavelli wrote. "This is because the conspirator always thinks that by killing the prince he will satisfy the people."

# Most Would Rather Follow a Leader Than Lead a Following

*When you are getting kicked from the rear,*
*it means you're in front.*
BISHOP FULTON J. SHEEN

History is replete with extreme examples of "followship." We may never fully understand how so many in Adolph Hitler's Germany could follow him into the depths of Hell or how cult leader Jim Jones persuaded 914 followers to join him in committing mass suicide. Most drank cyanide-laced Kool-Aid in 1978 at their "Jonestown" commune in Guyana. One lasting legacy of the Jonestown tragedy is a saying still heard to describe those who blindly follow a leader: "They drank the Kool-Aid," we say. It is often applied to situations that are incomparably less severe than the results in Jonestown. I heard it said many times in reference to the intensely devoted supporters of Democrat Howard Dean when he ran for president in 2004.

Whether drawn to evil, self-destruction, or simply the charisma of a well-intentioned political candidate, the instinct to follow dwells in most people. Some leaders arise because no one else wants to do the work. Church committees and condominium boards are full of such leaders. Give most people the option of letting someone else take the lead, and they will. And some people follow others to save themselves from their own poor judgment. In an episode of the television cartoon *King of the Hill*, the earnest Hank Hill worries that his bust-out neighborhood buddies have more fun when he isn't around to prevent them from doing stupid stuff. But by the end of the episode, Hank learns that his buddies really do like to have him in their midst, because they know that they need a parent figure to keep them out of trouble.

There is a pattern of codependency between leaders and followers. Leaders desire the power and influence that it brings. Followers prefer letting someone else make the tough decisions. If you decide to play the leader, you will need some technique. If you are a dedicated follower, you might need some protection.

Tapping into the human instinct to follow can bring great power to a leader, often with positive consequences for the followers. But unthinking indulgence of the desire to be led can bring disappointment.

Like many leadership positions, the American presidency is a model for the patterns and pitfalls of followership. Successful candidates typically begin by encouraging ridiculously naïve expectations among their followers. In covering White House races, I am often surprised at how readily some voters believe in grand promises.

Much of what presidential candidates promise is exceedingly beyond the powers of the office to ever achieve. And yet it has become a staple of modern campaigns to draft specific blueprints for a wide variety of detailed promises, usually without a single word dedicated to explaining how the candidate proposes to go about the most daunting task of all: persuading Congress to enact even a small part of the promised agenda.

No matter how many presidents come and go, failing to accomplish most of what they promise, the next crop of hopefuls finds a market of followers more than willing to suspend disbelief and expect the impossible.

## How to Build a Following

If you are an aspiring leader in any field, the lesson of presidential politics is to first make grand promises of what you will do for your potential followers. If you are a boss, you promise advancement to the workers. If you are a minister, you promise everlasting life. If you are a high school teacher, you promise the best colleges.

The next step in building a following is to make shining examples of those who fulfill your promises. If promoting a worker, do it with great fanfare, showing other employees what they can achieve by following you. If done meritoriously, these examples of success justify your role as leader, enhancing your power by keeping your followers convinced that they, too, will someday benefit from your leadership.

But if you continually grant success to those without merit, you will soon foster dissent that can threaten your position of leadership no matter how secure you think it might be. Punishment of dissent is a last resort in maintaining a following, usually made necessary by a failure of leadership. Still, the instinct to follow a leader is powerful enough in many people that it takes quite a lot to shake their support.

High school cliques and street gangs are crude examples of the need among insecure people to be part of something that they perceive as being bigger and better than themselves. Oddly, the young people who join cliques or gangs often think of themselves as shunning society's conventions—particularly, those of their parents—when in fact they are shunning their own individuality to meet the requirements of the group.

Disney's hit 2006 movie *High School Musical* features a signature song, "Stick to the Status Quo," that shows how kids pressure their peers. But the lyrics are not limited to high school: "If you wanna be cool, follow one simple rule. Don't mess with the flow, no no. Stick to the status quo."

The essence of successful leadership is to create a status quo that people want to stick to. Ideally, it is a status quo worth keeping. But even when it is not worth keeping, many follow anyway and bad things happen.

## FOLLOWING THE RIGHT LEADER CAN BE THE SMART CHOICE

The essence of successful followship is to pick your leaders well. For starters, do not be ashamed to put your faith in someone else to lead you. Most people are part follower and part leader. Few are purely one or the other.

Accepting leadership on occasion does not doom you to a life of submission. In my profession, I have seen many reporters resist editing. We call them "word proud." Some were good enough without it to get along quite well ignoring the advice of editors, but even a brilliant writer can make a mistake now and then. They end up having to write more corrections than do writers of lesser quality who paid attention to valid questions about their work before it was published. We all need a little protection from ourselves now and then. That is one of the things that a good leader offers to the flock.

Choose the right times to be a follower, but do not reject them all, or you will be setting yourself up for a burdensome life. Leading takes a lot of energy. Where do you fall on the continuum between blind follower and stubborn leader? One clue is to ask yourself if you are the kind of person who refuses under any circumstance to stop and ask for directions when you are lost. If so, you might be a bit too determined to make your own path when seeking a little help is in order. And you could end up wandering around completely lost.

On the other hand, if you are the type who makes no effort to navigate your own way, stopping in the middle of traffic to ask directions from anyone you see, then you might want to consider taking more responsibility for yourself.

Take the middle route. Ask for directions when your best-laid plans run afoul and you haven't got a clue where you're going. Even then, make intelligent choices about where you seek leadership. When driving in your car, the obvious sources of accurate information might be cab drivers, gas station attendants, or the police.

And so it is with the rest of life. Seek leadership when you need it, but pick the right people to get you where you are going. Refusing to accept leadership when you need it might keep you feeling in charge, but what good is that if there is nothing worthwhile to be in charge of? Leaders need a following to be leaders, and followers are not going to have much confidence in someone who is always going the wrong way because he could not bring himself to ask directions.

## Leaders Following the Followers

Careful leaders make a point of not getting too far ahead of their following or risk losing them altogether. These are the ones who illustrate Bishop Fulton J. Sheen's observation that getting kicked from behind proves you are in front.

The flipside of Sheen's quote is that a leader who is close enough to kick is a leader who will listen to you. Perhaps that is a good definition of democracy, a system where the leaders are always close enough for the public to kick them around.

In a democracy, elected officials follow opinion polls and other measurements of public opinion in hopes of staying popular enough to stay in office. There is a downside, however. What if the public is actually wrong about what is best for them?

Civil rights legislation was a long time coming in the United States simply because the voting public for generations rejected political candidates who supported it—which is why Lyndon Johnson was so depressed, according to aides, on the night in 1964 when his push for civil rights laws finally won enough votes in Congress to be enacted. He correctly worried that his party, the Democrats, would be badly damaged by the loss of voters against the legislation.

Johnson was well ahead of the public on that night, always a dangerous place to be. And sure enough, the Democrats are still trying to rebuild the dominance that they had enjoyed in the South before the civil rights era dawned.

# Those Who Prefer to Lead a Following Cannot Be Trusted

*Wherever there is a man who exercises authority,*
*there is a man who resists authority.*
OSCAR WILDE

Never trust leaders unless you are firmly in the majority of their crowd. And even then, be careful. Unless you stand to benefit from the aims of a leader, it is not worth joining the crowd.

Wherever a following rallies around a leader, somebody tends to be left out. Too often, it seems, the purpose of a group is to exclude those who do not belong. Devious leaders know this, encouraging their members to discriminate against nonmembers as a way of reinforcing loyalty to the group. Religious charlatans have long exploited this dynamic of human nature, rallying the faithful against nonbelievers.

You have to wonder if human history might have been less violent if there were no heroes around to persuade followers to do their bidding. As the title song from the apocalyptic film *Thunderdome* puts it, "We don't need another hero."

Heroic leaders belong in myths and movies, but once they turn up in real life, things do not always turn out so well.

Alexander the Great was a powerful leader, but he also got a lot of people killed.

Even leaders who ask for little sacrifice from their followers sometimes disappoint them. Among professional sports figures, those with feet of clay seem to have become the rule rather than the exception.

Beware the people in your life who want to form a group or lead a cause. Carefully consider what they are looking to get out of the situation. There are few with purely good and selfless purposes in mind—bless them all.

Even the leaders of families are sometimes not trustworthy, using their children or mates to aggrandize themselves. Joan Crawford made a public spectacle of her children, more determined that her fans see her as an exemplary mother than she was about giving them love and affection offstage. Men who marry only to impress society are said to take on "trophy wives."

## LEADING WITH PERCEPTION

Leaders tend to dwell on the appearance of things, knowingly or unknowingly heeding Machiavelli's observation that "humans generally judge more by what they see, rather than what they feel, and everyone sees what you seem to be, but few perceive what you are."

Despite their flaws and dangers, I suppose that we need leaders. We might all still be huddled in caves eating leaves if somebody had not led us to better lives. But my guess is that the first caveman leader ended up taking better care of himself than the rest of the group. And the crowd most likely turned on him.

Too cynical? Perhaps. But there are many examples of heroes being deposed by their own foolishness to ignore the possibility. Hans Christian Andersen's fairy-tale emperor was so into himself that he was easily duped into thinking that he could wear nothing at all and parade down the street as his subjects bowed and worshipped his glorious "wardrobe." It worked for a while until someone pointed out that the emperor was wearing no clothes. The moral of this Danish fairy tale might caution us to be neither a foolish emperor nor a foolish follower. Even if the crowd believes in the pretensions of its leader, that does not make them true. And sooner or later somebody is bound to see through the façade.

If you are determined to be a leader, give your potential followers something genuine and uplifting to support. Follow through with results that demonstrate your honesty. If you base your leadership on a lie or false promises, you will be found out.

Sure, plenty of leaders get away with their fraudulent ways for a long time. To paraphrase Mark Twain, a lie can circle the globe many times while the truth is still putting its pants on.

Machiavelli offers guidance to the devious leader whose intentions are not selfless. Such leaders should still exhibit the qualities of "mercy, faithfulness, integrity, and kindness." It is not important "to have" these great qualities, Machiavelli advised, but it is important "to appear" to have them, and "should it become necessary not to be so, the wise ruler will be able and know how to change to the contrary." Indeed, Machiavelli suggests that successful leaders are better off only appearing to be good and decent, for he believed that, "when necessity commands it," a strong leader "should know how to enter into evil."

While shockingly heartless advice, Machiavelli's guidance is often heeded, even by the most benign-appearing leaders. In the mid-1970s, a congressional investigation of the CIA uncovered various examples of the intelligence agency's illegal spying on Americans and several attempts to assassinate foreign leaders such as Cuba's Fidel Castro. The Church Committee—named for its chairman, Senator Frank Church, an Idaho Democrat—condemned the CIA but also concluded that past presidents had condoned or authorized the illegal actions.

While not all of the Church Committee's findings three decades ago have been declassified, the 50,000 pages that have been made public read like pages taken directly from Machiavelli's text. In affairs of state there is no room for a leader to act morally at all times. Victory at any cost was his maxim. And in the Church Committee's unprecedented exposure of government's shadowy underworld, we learned just how Machiavellian the leaders of a modern democracy could behave four centuries after he set forth his maxim that evil actions should be used "when necessity commands it."

## Neither Caesar nor Brutus Be

If you would rather lead than follow, be suspicious of potential rivals. Machiavelli advises that if you are newly installed in your position of power, you quickly take stock of those who had unsuccessfully vied for the power conferred upon you. He starts by citing the example of Caesar, the Roman emperor ultimately assassinated by rivals whom he had failed to eliminate. "He who establishes a tyranny and does not kill Brutus, and he who establishes a democratic regime and does not kill the sons of Brutus, will not last long," Machiavelli said.

It might be tempting to befriend your rivals and make them part of your kingdom. Caesar tried that and they killed him. If the man who rose to rule most of the known world in his day could not pull it off, how can you?

This is one of the most challenging dilemmas that leaders face. They need strong and capable associates to carry their will forward, but these are often the same people who cannot be trusted to remain loyal. Ultimately, they want the leader's job.

While it could make for a less efficient organization, the leader's power will be more secure if surrounded by less ambitious associates who are as competent as possible. They do not have to be as kowtowing as Mr. Burns's pathetic aide Smithers in *The Simpsons*, but Mr. Burns knows better than to take on someone who might want to own his nuclear plant someday.

Large bureaucracies, in government and in the private world, tend to be better homes for followers than leaders. That is no accident. Those who want to make their own way in the world are not the personality type that such organizations seek. If you are that type, it is fine to spend time in a corporate or governmental bureaucracy, but you better have your exit strategy in mind when the time comes for you to build your own thing. Otherwise, you are going to have to play Brutus somewhere down the road if you intend to become number one in a bureaucracy. Figuratively speaking, you will probably have to assassinate somebody to get the job. And whomever that might be is probably someone who knows the drill because that is how he or she got there in the first place.

Playing Brutus in this situation is tough work, and it most likely calls for a lifetime commitment that could leave you with nothing if you fail. Better to just get out and start your own company or run for political office yourself.

## Balance Your Inner Leader and Follower

Oscar Wilde put the nature of authority and resistance into stark relief, saying that for all who exert authority there is someone to resist it. Such absolutist language on this subject is not too surprising from someone who nearly died in jail for resisting the cultural and moral authority of his times.

The tension between authoritarianism and resistance exists within most people. Dictatorial tendencies and at least the hint of a protestor's soul coexist within most people. More plainly put, there is a leader and a follower in all of us. Choosing which to be should not be a matter of excluding the other for the rest of life. Sometimes our families, schools, or workplaces try to cram us into being a lifelong leader or a lifelong follower. Too many of us accept this conditioning, overlooking the moments in life when we ought to switch roles.

There are situations when we should step forward and take the lead, and there are others when we should shut up and take a backseat.

## Never Seek a Favor That Could Cost Too Much to Return

*Favor and honor sometimes fall more fitly*
*on those who do not desire them.*
Titus Livius

Favors are pleasant but dangerous. Owing a favor to someone diminishes your control. Collecting payback for favors can get nasty. As with promises, keep track of the favors that you owe as much as those that you hand out.

I knew someone once who offered lots of favors but never without a price—and the price often was costlier than the benefit of the favor. Even the simple offer of a ride somewhere came at the cost of helping load the car with heavy boxes that needed moving. It would have been easier to walk to my destination.

For some people, everything is commerce. They are masters at getting what they want while managing to make the other person feel obligated to them. Even those who do not ask that favors be paid back can be getting something in return. They might give to charity in return for the accolades showered upon their generosity, or they might simply want to be loved or befriended by those they favor.

In most cases, seeking or granting favors is a quasi-business transaction. I had a friend in college who kept a written record whenever doing a favor for someone, no matter how minor—and there was always a return price sought. We teased my college friend mercilessly about this behavior and engaged in elaborate, often comically drawn-out negotiations for class notes, a little cash, or anything else of perceived value. It was probably good preparation for the transactional negotiations of adulthood.

Clever favor givers do not only seek something of equal value as payback. They require a premium, something of value beyond that of the favor granted. Why? Because in truth they usually do not have to grant the favor, so they want to be paid a "fee" for agreeing to the transaction in the first place.

If you are at lunch, for instance, suddenly realizing that you have lost your wallet or forgotten to pay off your credit card and your lunch mate graciously agrees to pay the bill, do not just pay back the exact amount when you can. Pay for both meals, as a premium for getting you out of an embarrassing situation.

Expecting favors from others and only returning the exact value of what they gave will earn you a lousy reputation, even if they never confront you directly about it, which is why it is best to ask only for favors that you can afford to pay back in kind with a little extra on top. If you cannot afford this, do not ask for the favor.

Banks do not loan money without collecting interest. If the borrower had to pay back only the principal, the bank would make no profit. The interest is charged as a premium for the lender's agreement to do business with the borrower.

Likewise, do not readily hand out too many favors without an adequate return price. Sometimes, charity is no gift at all because the recipients of your generosity never learn to take care of themselves. This happens quite often among family members, or it might cause the borrower of your goodwill or resources to lose respect for you and abuse your kindness. Then you might get mad, break off relations, and end up having created an enemy in your life simply because you were trying to be helpful.

## EQUITABLE TRANSACTIONS MAKE GOOD RELATIONS

Whether asking for favors or receiving them, keeping good relations depends on an equitable transaction.

What if a friend, or even just a friend of a friend, asks you to introduce him or her to an influential person in your circle because he or she wants to propose a business deal or ask for a job? This is a fairly common occurrence in the working world. Should you trouble your powerful associate—and risk making that person less receptive to your own requests later on—for nothing in return?

Amazingly, many people ask for such favors and expect to give you only a token gift, a free lunch, or maybe nothing at all. You might agree to do the favor on the expectation that at some point in the future he or she will do you a similar favor if you need it. Do not count on it. Favors not returned in a timely fashion are favors ultimately forgotten.

Once you have analyzed the many pitfalls of asking for a favor and determined that it must be sought, carefully consider how to ask. Do not be flippant about asking for a favor, and first ask yourself if the request is reasonable.

Choose a conducive location and time for a serious conversation. Ask the person for permission to talk, making sure it is convenient. Look at the person directly, being clear and specific about what you are asking for and what you are offering in return for the favor.

If you are being asked for a favor, be wary of anyone who does not show respect for your intelligence. Many people ask for favors indirectly, as though they are not even asking for a favor at all but rather presenting you with a situation in which any decent person would agree to what they are seeking. These are the people who are the least likely to make your favor worth giving.

## BEWARE THE FAVOR-SEEKING CON ARTIST

You know that there is manipulation afoot when someone says, "Can you do me a favor?" Even worse when he or she says, "Do you promise not to get mad?" In both cases the favor asker might be planning to ask for something of yours that you are not obligated to give, or the person might be preparing to tell you something that he or she has already done that you would never have agreed to before that person did it.

By asking such questions, some people, mindful that you are under no obligation to them, are trying to make you obligated by getting your agreement to do something even before you know what it is. Talk about a setup. It is a good bet that you are about to be played for the fool when anyone asks such scheming questions. Even a close friend or family member should be placed under suspicion when approaching you in this way.

I got a lesson in this routine when I was about eight years old. A neighborhood friend who was around my age would ask, "Can you do me a favor?" I would say yes, and then he would ask for something of mine, usually a toy or whatever kids value at that age. If I said no, he would get mad, arguing that I had said that I would do him a favor. He did not get away with this often in our neighborhood but often enough that he kept trying and would take possession of more than he deserved. Of course, I quickly learned to say no when he would set me up in this way.

Ever since those days, I think of that kid when somebody asks for a favor before saying what the favor is. Usually, it is something that people say when they know that they are asking for too much. And, yet, I often see people fall into the trap.

Persistent favor seekers prey upon the goodwill of others. They know that most people want to seem agreeable and will positively respond. Do not fall for it. An easy comeback to "Can you do me a favor?" is "What is it?" or "Not until you tell me what it is." Or, if you suspect brazen manipulation, call it out. Say to the person, "That is a manipulative question; try again." This might put them off guard, and, realizing you are not such an easy mark, they might abandon asking you for the favor at all.

## The Clever Favor Seeker Does Not Even Ask

You will give up less to receive favors from others if you do not specifically ask for the favor. This is how I interpret Titus Livius, the ancient Roman historian who said that those who do not desire favor and honor are more fit to receive them. Livius was making a larger point about the benefits of humility, but it is good advice, even for those who are not so humble. The appearance of being someone who is not seeking a favor can be an effective way to receive favors that you secretly want.

Watch out for the clever types who understand this. It might be someone who plays the quiet martyr, vaguely mentioning something that he or she always wanted or needed but could not afford—in hopes that you will pick up the hint and give it to him or her. People like this know that if you can make a gift or favor someone else's idea, the giver will be even more enthusiastic and it will cost you nothing in return. Or it might be someone who knows how to give very little for a big payoff. A coworker brings you a new coffee cup with the really big handle that you like—and then just happens to mention that he or she needs some help on a big project. If you are not careful, you could end up working an entire weekend and get nothing but a $2 coffee cup in return.

## Leading the Way for
## Change Seldom Pays

*Change is upsetting. Repetition is tedious.*
*Three cheers for variation!*
MASON COOLEY

Martin Luther King Jr. and Gandhi are dead. That was their payback for being agents of change. Not everyone ends up gunned down for trying to change the world, but change agents usually do not fare well.

Most people go along to get along, accepting injustice and indignity as the price for survival. Society advances when a Reverend King or a Gandhi comes along, which is why each richly deserved to be lionized in death. But they still died prematurely, and anyone following their path must be prepared for a similar fate.

To keep power—or to stay alive—the political player is better off steering a course of moderation between the status quo and radical change. Become too protective of the status quo and you risk an uprising by those seeking change. Embrace dramatic change and you risk reprisals from believers in the status quo. Even the most peaceful change agents, such as King and Gandhi, sometimes meet violent endings.

Sure, moderation is not exciting. It is a lousy rallying cry for a crowd, but it keeps you in control. The trick is in staying on top of change but not in front of it. And even when change is accepted, it can easily be undercut by the overconfidence of those who achieved it and the unrelenting opposition from those who fought against it.

Senator John McCain's long-suffering battle for campaign finance reform in Washington, D.C., demonstrates Machiavelli's point that "the innovator has against him those who benefited from the old system; while those who should benefit from the new are only lukewarm friends." In the end, the Arizona Republican's 2002 legislative victory did little to stem the tide of big money in American politics. Loopholes were soon found, and at best his legislation redirected the flow a bit but did little to change the system. And yet, McCain continues to get political credit for at least trying to be a reformer. In some ways, the equivocal results of his efforts put him in a stronger position than if he had completely succeeded. He earned the title of reformer but did not actually change anything enough to make lifelong enemies of the keepers of the status quo.

## REAL CHANGE REQUIRES GOOD PLANNING

It is better politics to play the role of an innovator without actually changing things too much. If you are determined to really change things, you will need plenty of firepower. Throughout history, armed agents of change enjoyed longer lives than did the unarmed.

Sometimes change is absolutely necessary. As a boss, you might be faced with needing to reduce your company's contribution to the employee pension plan or health program. If not, your company risks going bankrupt. Parents might need to prepare their children for an impending divorce or a far-away move to take a new job. Children often face the need to tell their parents unsettling news.

The techniques for successfully leading the way to change are roughly similar whether preparing a nation for societal upheaval or adjusting your family to something new. First, you need a plan. Never spring ill-formed ideas for change on others. The natural human resistance to change will overwhelm you. The status quo always enjoys a tactical advantage, simply because it already exists. Change is nothing but an idea until it is actually implemented. Imaginations run wild about the potentially harmful consequences of change, and without preparation you will not be able to respond convincingly. Analyze every possible reaction to your proposal for change before you bring it up. The initial human reaction to change usually begins with denial and then quickly shifts into anger and resistance.

If you are ready with a quick and persuasive response to the denial of any need for change, you have a chance to control the conversation before anger and resistance set in. If not, you are going to have a tough time winning your struggle for change.

It is best to preempt the denial reaction by opening the discussion with a detailed and convincing case for the need to make changes. Do this before you introduce your own proposals. Rarely will this win the day on its own, but it ideally puts you on a constructive path. People respond more positively to change if they first understand and recognize the problem that you are addressing.

Once you have achieved as much understanding as possible of the problem at hand, present your proposal for change as a "tentative" plan. It might be helpful to outline alternatives. If it is feasible to give others a role in choosing among the alternatives, do so. Giving others some ownership of the solutions can dramatically ease the path to change. Make it clear that you are well aware of the reasons that some might resist your ideas. Show the resistors that you respect their concerns and that you are struggling to accommodate them.

Once you have presented your tentative outline for change, let it rest for a time. Announcing your final decision in the first conversation all but guarantees a difficult path filled with anger and resistance. In the initial discussion, it is better to establish a timetable for reaching a final decision.

Allowing people time to explore the problem that you have defined and to ponder the consequences of the change that you have proposed will greatly improve the chances that they will ultimately reach acceptance. Once they accept change, quickly implement it, and, if you have patiently done your homework, they might even bond with your changes.

## Computers Leading the Way to Change

Human reaction to change is so predictable that computer scientists are exploring ways to automate the conditioning of people to accept change. At Stanford University these experts call this *captology*, a body of expertise in "the design, theory, and analysis of persuasive technologies." The purpose of this scientific project is to design computer models for changing attitudes in many areas, including health, business, safety, and education. For instance, the Stanford team studies how to use mobile devices, such as cell phones and other handheld computers, to guide people through a series of steps to quit smoking and monitor their progress.

On the dark side, this technology is perfecting the use of video games in military training to modify attitudes toward killing, desensitizing trainees and making them more receptive to the violence of warfare. "For the target population—young males—nothing manipulates better or faster than video games," a Stanford study concluded.

Persuasion via computer technology is no different than human-to-human persuasion. Indeed, these computer models are based on successful techniques from the nonvirtual world. Computers simply help monitor and encourage people through the stages of change.

Make your call for change as entertaining as possible. People respond more positively if they are enjoying themselves, trying something new presented in a familiar and entertaining format. Take your employees on a pleasant retreat or even a special lunch if you need to raise an idea that might meet resistance.

Repeated exposure to a new concept or experience makes it more and more familiar. You want to reach a point where the change is no longer change at all, where people become used to what was once different to them. It is remarkable how often you will find that they almost forget that they were once used to something else. If you have properly led the way to change, you will find that they resist any suggestion to go back to their old ways.

Monitoring the progress of change and providing constant feedback helps people work through a tough transition. Just barking out orders and waiting for everyone to adjust will not be effective. You need to find ways to show progress each step along the way, just as parents put a mark on the kitchen door for growing children to see their rising height.

It takes lot of planning and effort—and a lot of handholding—to smoothly change what people believe or how they behave. When following the lead of computer captologists, it is important to devise as many ways as possible to give people incremental exposure to what is new to them, constant feedback on their progress, and clear measurement of their progress.

Guide others to change. Do not just demand it.


## Aim for the Center

Mason Cooley was a renowned aphorist, author of witty sayings with a message. The Staten Island College professor penned a worthy line in proclaiming, "Three cheers for variation!"

Change is upsetting and repetition is tedious. But give people some variety between the two extremes, and they are more likely to follow your lead. The middle ground is considered safe for a reason. Most people fear radical change but do not want to fall into a rut.

In political campaigns, this mantra transforms into a call for "moderation," a code word for the ideological center. Both Democrats and Republicans often face political trouble if they are seen as being too aligned with the "extreme" wings of their parties.

In 1992, Bill Clinton ran for president as a Southern moderate. In 2000, George W. Bush called for "compassionate conservatism." In both cases they were signaling to voters that they were not captives of those in their parties who advocated frightening change. But they were also showing that they were on a new path, not bound by the boring repetition of past standard-bearers for their respective parties.

You could say that Clinton and Bush won the presidency partly by echoing Cooley's mantra "Three cheers for variation!"

# Wanting Power Requires Less Intelligence Than Seeking Power

*Power is action.*
HONORÉ DE BALZAC

Look no further than Deputy Barney Fife and Sheriff Andy Taylor for the difference between wanting power and actually getting it. There are many reasons why *The Andy Griffith Show*, which first aired in the early 1960s, has survived in reruns for more than forty-five years. But a major reason is the comical and telling contrast in styles between the leading characters, played by Don Knotts and Andy Griffith.

Knotts's Barney Fife was an extreme example of someone desperately wanting power but being completely without the intelligence to achieve it. Griffith's character can well be the most effective leader ever created for film or television. Griffith's Andy Taylor ruled Mayberry with a soft touch. He could referee petty disputes among the quirky residents of his fictional North Carolina town with humor and empathy, raising his voice only on those rare occasions when it became necessary. He could subdue the bad guys by outwitting them and by doing so without a gun.

"When a man carries a gun all the time, the respect he thinks he's getting might really be fear," Sheriff Taylor said in one episode. "So I don't carry a gun, because I don't want the people of Mayberry to fear a gun. I'd rather they respect me." Andy was the most intelligent and powerful person in his domain but seldom let it show.

Deputy Fife was Sheriff Taylor's complete opposite. Frantically desiring the power to boss around the townsfolk, he loved to carry a gun but was so inept at handling it that Andy would not let him have any bullets. In one of the show's most hysterical episodes, Andy leaves town for a day, putting Barney in charge as acting sheriff. Upon returning, he discovers that his overzealous deputy has arrested dozens of the townspeople for minor infractions. Andy dismisses all of the charges, and Barney's power trip is over.

Many who desire power cannot be trusted with the ammunition that it takes to actually get it and hold onto it long enough to remain in charge. Even those with the smarts to handle power over others should seek it only when absolutely necessary.

Seeking power—and finding it—is a lot of work. Maintaining power requires even more diligence. Enemies are likely to be made. Choose carefully when you must have control. Once the path is chosen, power must be pursued with intelligence and care.


## Aim High When They're Riding Horses

It is vital to win power once you decide to seek it. Failed power plays can be disastrous. As the saying goes, when the enemy is riding horses, be sure to aim high.

The elements of seeking power begin with considering whether anyone else already has the power you seek. If so, will that person share power? Not likely, unless you devise a reason why doing so would somehow enhance his or her status.

If you must seize power from someone else against his or her will, you have your work cut out for you. For starters you must operate without that person's knowledge. You cannot afford to let the target know what you are up to until you have enough leverage to defend yourself against counterattacks.

Power plays are best accomplished with extensive planning and lightning-fast execution. The longer it takes to implement, the more likely that unexpected obstacles emerge.

Identify potential associates who might benefit from your rise to power and be willing to provide crucial assistance. Carefully consider whether they can be trusted. Even if you conclude that they are completely trustworthy, do not tell them everything that you are planning. Only tell them what they need to know to make their contribution to your plan. The more anyone knows of your plans, the less control you will have over what others might learn of it.

Once power is secured, you are not finished. Anyone who might be disadvantaged by your success is a potential threat to your maintaining power. Examine whether they can be co-opted to your side with a generous display of your newfound power that benefits them in some way. Any chance of turning an enemy into a friend should be explored.

The best power plays are those that evolve along a natural course that seem completely unplanned to the casual observer. Andy Griffith's television sheriff was a master at this, using his knack for persuasion and suggestion—and lots of reverse psychology—to move others along a path that often seemed to them as a course of their own making.

Of course, Andy Taylor was a fictional character who was always trying to do the right thing and pursue what was best for the town as a whole. Some power plays in the real world benefit only those in charge, making such plays much tougher to win and exceedingly difficult to maintain.

It is more promising for real-life power players to seek positive goals that benefit as many people as possible. The more who benefit, the less you will have to worry about insurgencies against your power. This often means that the power seeker must be generous with the spoils of victory. Better to give up some of the winnings than to risk losing everything.

## THE LESSONS OF SADDAM

Saddam Hussein was just plain stupid or crazy, or both. Sure, he had the intelligence to win control of Iraq and maintain power for a long time. But in the end he was undone by his own crude and brutal methods as well as his foolish mishandling of the United States. His countrymen were quite willing to see him go, which is a major reason that U.S. forces so quickly removed him from power in 2003.

Of course, U.S. troops were not long greeted as "liberators," as the Bush administration had so confidently predicted. Before long, the United States became seen as an occupying force. Still, my guess is that most Iraqis would not trade the American presence for a return to Hussein's regime.

Hussein is a most extreme example of an evil dictator making mistakes that many decent people make in trying to hold on to their power. His central error was in pretending to have weapons of mass destruction that, while keeping his neighboring enemies at bay, served to invite an American invasion that cost him everything.

Here are a few of the lessons that even the most benign power seekers might learn from Hussein.

- Making threats to frighten rivals can backfire. Someone else might just call your bluff, and that someone could be more powerful than you.

- Miscalculating your enemies' actions is a frequent failing of the unintelligent leader. Better to assume the worst than be surprised. Carefully prepare for an all-out assault against you, and the odds of survival improve.

- Avoid conflict with those who are more powerful. Pick your fights carefully—preferably, just one at a time. Take on the whole world, and you do not have much of a chance to survive.

- Never taunt a more powerful foe if you do not have the means to back it up. You might provoke a response that never would have occurred if you had kept your mouth shut.

- Do not take too much advantage of those with less power. Treat them with respect, even when you are taking advantage of them. Be as generous as possible. Sharing some power with weaker associates poses little threat and goes a long way toward keeping them mostly in your camp. Otherwise, you will drive them into the arms of a stronger force than you can handle.

The Roman Empire came up with a brilliant ploy to keep weaker peoples at bay. They offered them Roman citizenship, or a least a scaled-down version. In many cases, the prospects and benefits of this offer encouraged some to lay down their arms and surrender without a fight.

Saddam might have survived in power with a bit more generosity to his neighbors, less cruelty to his own people, and a more realistic approach to the United States. But then, if he was indeed as crazy as he seems, such tactics were never in the cards for him.

## POWER MUST BE SEEN TO BE BELIEVED

Political power is much like electrical power. You cannot see it, but its effects are quite visible. Talking about your power without showing it will persuade few people that you really have it. They might even assume that you are "all talk and no action." Or, as they say about fake cowboys, "all hat and no cattle."

Power is action, as Balzac said. It must be turned on to be effective. People notice results more than promises. If they see your power in action, they believe that it exists. But that does not mean that you must burn the lights of your power all day and all night to persuade people that you have it.

When we turn off our electricity, we assume it is still there. We also know that if we use too much, the local power plant could shut down.

Conserve you power and use it wisely so that you never run out of juice.

# Those Who Are Dependent on You Will Be the Most Faithful

*The sadistic person is as dependent on the submissive
person as the latter is on the former.*
Erich Fromm

Dependency is the narcotic of power. The powerless depend on the powerful. But the powerful also depend on their dependents. Codependency is not just for substance abusers and their families.

In the mental health world, codependency is considered a disorder, an emotional and behavioral condition that affects an individual's ability to have a healthy, mutually satisfying relationship. It is often the most telling sign of a dysfunctional family.

Power politics cannot function without dependency. If followers do not depend on the powerful for leadership, there is only chaos. Likewise, the successful leader must depend on the followers to follow.

Followers should carefully choose their leaders. Remember what parents tell children who succumb to peer pressure? If your pal jumped off a cliff, would you follow?

Some people would jump. Look at cult leaders such as David Koresh, whose followers stuck with him to their fiery deaths in the federal assault on their compound in Waco, Texas.

Society needs "followship" to maintain order, but, as in most things, there are limits—and sometimes the followers should critically question the wisdom of their leader's path.

Successful leaders must cultivate dependency to ensure a faithful following. This makes the follower's submission a matter of necessity instead of choice. Those who merely choose to follow without any particular need to do so cannot be trusted to remain faithful when the going gets rough.

Cultivating dependency is easy for a boss who controls the paychecks. There is no better way to win the hearts and minds of most people than to target their wallets. Politicians know this. Whether cutting taxes or handing out federal dollars, they are always mindful of the power derived from putting money into the pockets of voters.

Before becoming president, Lyndon Johnson built a career on distributing federal largesse to rural Texans, literally turning their lights on by expanding access to electricity. He also perfected the political science of placing military bases and other defense projects in vote-rich areas. Johnson did not discover these techniques, but he certainly took them to greater heights.

## The Downside of Economic Dependency

Economic dependency is probably the most effective tool for building a faithful following, but it also can be the most tenuous. Parents use the allowance to reinforce a child's dependency on them. My own parents happened to disagree with this approach. My father, an employer himself, was against turning his child into a pseudo-employee, saying that if there was something that I wanted or needed, we would decide as a family whether it fit the overall budget. I never felt economically dependent on my parents (though I was) but, instead, owed allegiance to them out of something much stronger, an emotional bond of love and respect that comes right out of my childhood experience as part of an integral family.

A parent who lords over a child with economic threats ensures the day when the offspring breaks the bond, usually on the day that first real paycheck is cashed. Plenty of successful earners will tell you that they owe their success to their eagerness to break free of domineering parents. So in that way, the parents' methods encouraged the child to be successful, but they lost the family bond along the way. And so it is in most power plays.

Cultivate dependency based exclusively on something tangible—a child's allowance, a worker's paycheck, or free drinks for your friends—and you might find yourself alone once the tangible thing is gone or they find somewhere else to get it.

The most successful leaders also build faith on the intangibles. Empathy is an effective tool for encouraging followers. Bill Clinton was famous for "I feel your pain," a phrase summing up his remarkable skill at making voters feel as though he woke up every day worrying about the same things they did.

Despite belonging to a different political party and standing worlds apart from Clinton on the issues, Ronald Reagan had a similar knack. If anything, Reagan was even better at it because he was more subtle, never going so far with the empathy routine that it became a joking matter, as it did with

Clinton. Regardless of that, both demonstrated a genuine knack for reaching middle-class Americans by convincingly demonstrating empathy for them.

A longtime Reagan adviser, Michael Deaver, was once asked how Reagan seemed to understand intrinsically how to turn a phrase or spin an anecdote that aligned him so well with average Americans, even though he had lived his entire adult life in the rarified world of movies and politics. Deaver answered with an example from Reagan's White House routine. He said that on most nights, the president and his wife, Nancy, preferred to sit at home in the mansion's upstairs family quarters watching prime-time television and eating dinner from TV trays.

Deaver's answer was deceptively simple. Some might even find it to be a flippant nonanswer. But in Washington I have often noticed that career politicians have no clue what most Americans are watching on television every night. Reagan had found a remarkably obvious way to stay in touch, and yet to this day I do not think most leaders spend a nanosecond paying attention to what their voters are really seeing on a daily basis.

## THE CODEPENDENT BLUES

Look at how many rock stars grew to hate each other but stayed together in their bands for the record sales? Van Halen comes to mind. Others split up and were never heard from again. A few individuals returned to the pop charts without their founding partners.

Similarly, what do we do when an association with someone else is quite profitable but the psychic costs of putting up with him or her start running high? It is not uncommon for people who work so closely together to build a great success and end up being sick of each other, simply because they spent so much time together. This does not just happen to celebrity musicians. It is common for law firms, family businesses, and college roommates.

The temptation is to chuck it all and go out on your own. Sometimes it works, but often it does not. When faced with a difficult but extremely successful association, approach it like a divorce. Is it truly irreconcilable? Or is there a chance that a bit of humility and compromise could keep you both on the winning track? Some do not even ask these questions before they bolt.

People who depend on each other can easily grow tired of the codependency. But if the product of that codependency is profitable, they should give it a lot of thought before giving up.

The graveyard of forgotten singers is full of those who thought that they did not need their original bands anymore, but there are some who made it—Sting comes to mind, as do Peter Gabriel and Don Henley (though the latter still reunites with other members of the Eagles for reunion shows). Deciding whether it is time to be your own star and end a successful partnership should be carefully considered and never rashly made in a fit of anger or jealousy.

Be straightforward with yourself about others whom you might depend on. Resist the tendency to think that you are independent of them, until you are positive that you have made an accurate assessment. Strong-willed people who must depend on one another naturally resist the dependency on occasion.

The codependency breakup happens in presidential politics. Look at Bill Clinton and Al Gore. They needed each other and their wives in 1992 to present a winning image of baby-boomer couples who attracted many voters. George Herbert Walker Bush and his vice president, Dan Quayle, built a less equal partnership, and the elder Bush ultimately showed no interest in allowing Quayle to get a promotion. He naturally supported his own son, George W. Bush, in the 2000 race and ignored Quayle's bid.

The list goes on and on. In presidential politics, as in most things, the higher the stakes for a partnership and the more the partners depend on each other, the greater the chance that someday the whole thing falls apart.

## You Are at Risk When the
## Powerful Depend on You

Erich Fromm's quote on the codependency among sadistic and submissive people illustrates a phenomenon that occurs in less extreme situations. The back-and-forth dependency in power relationships plays out in many settings. Look at how even the greatest presidents depended on effective chiefs of staff to do their bidding and implement their decisions. Usually, when a president's public support falters, the chief of staff is blamed and is the first to go. The chief of staff depends on the president to keep the job because the president is conversely so dependent on that person to keep control of the White House itself.

Beware getting into a codependent relationship with a powerful person. It might seem like a good thing. It makes you feel powerful to have this person relying on you. But it could be awful for your job security. You could be better off a few notches below, in a position that is not too close to the top—if you want to keep your job, that is.

The more a powerful person depends on you, the more at risk you are. If things go bad, you are the first to be let go.

# A True Enemy Should Be Eliminated, Never Tolerated

*Our enemy is by tradition our savior,*
*in preventing us from superficiality.*
JOYCE CAROL OATES

When competitive skateboarders decide to outdo a rival, they say that it is time to "take out the trash." Sometimes in life you might think that you need to make an enemy to achieve your goal—that there is no way around such a path.

Think again. Be sure that there is no other way. Never make an enemy by choice. Do it only when necessary. If you have a choice about whether to make an enemy, choose against it. I have seen many people lose their power—or their jobs—by making enemies instead of friends. If you really do not have a choice and decide that the only option is to burn the bridge to an adversary, prepare to wage all-out war. There is probably no turning back once you have declared war.

War at home or at the office differs little from war between nations. Uncompromising enemies should be rare, but if and when they come along, your assault should be well planned and your endgame firmly in mind. It is much easier to start a war than to end it.

I have made few enemies in life (that I know of), and in nearly every case it could have been avoided had I realized it at the time. In one of my stints as a manager, I encountered the head of another department whose hostility and sour attitude seriously affected my unit. I tried every imaginable way to get along. But my schmoozing got nowhere and even seemed to make this person think that I was a softie who could be rolled over.

There is some danger in going the extra mile to befriend a potential adversary, but you have to try. Some people mistake friendliness for weakness, becoming even more belligerent. I really cannot stand such people. They allow so few options for ways to maintain civil relations.

Rare is the person who cannot be disarmed with a smile and friendly word. But unfortunately they do exist, and I found such a person at the office where I once worked. For weeks I deployed every imaginable pleasantry that I could muster, only to be met with defiant resistance at every turn.

I finally exploded in a poorly planned episode that got us nowhere. This person had sent yet another nasty e-mail to my entire workforce about some petty complaint. Grabbing a printout, I marched over and started yelling like a crazy person. This, of course, made me look like the hothead.

Losing your temper against an enemy will backfire unless it is a well-considered tactic within a carefully planned strategy. It allows the other person to play it cool, presenting the face of reason to those around you—no matter how much your diatribe was justifiably provoked by the other person.

You know the type: someone who insults you and then, after you get visibly angry, says, "Hey, I was just kidding." And you look like the fool who cannot take a joke.

## STAY COOL WHEN PROVOKING OTHERS

War against an enemy should be waged as an extension of politics. Keep open to opportunities for negotiating a cease-fire. Escalate hostilities only when they are escalated against you. Define your rules of engagement. Anticipate your adversaries' responses as best you can, and decide in advance how you will counter them. Losing sight of your rules of engagement can lead to chaos and possibly defeat.

I followed none of this advice in my sudden eruption against my office adversary. We ended up never speaking to each other again, which led to many difficulties and inefficiencies for both of us. If I had followed a more graduated series of escalations, we might have found common ground long before I blew up the bridge between us.

Incrementally stepping up hostilities against a foe allows you to force the other person to choose his or her weapons and reveal the jerk that he or she probably is. It helps you look more reasonable to onlookers if they plainly see your adversary's hostile behavior. People tend to focus on the drama of someone's emotional behavior and less upon the subtle provocations that brought it about.

Ideally, you want to provoke the other side to an emotional outburst, allowing you to play it cool and emerge as the face of reason. This is victory—or at least it will be in the eyes of those who are watching. Undermining a foe in the minds of others will go a long way toward putting you in the superior position.

True enemies simply cannot be tolerated when your own power and prestige are at stake. Once such a foe is identified and all other options are ruled out, victory must be pursued with intelligence and determination. This is why taking on enemies should be avoided if at all possible. Taking out the trash is dirty work.

## Keep a Close Watch on Your Enemies List

Never take on an enemy for the joy of it. Amazingly, some people relish a fight. They seldom get ahead. No one wants to work with them or even be around them. Yet they persist in aggravating people.

A classmate in high school was one of these people. In what he apparently thought was good-natured teasing, I guess, this guy made a habit of offending people and tearing them down whenever they accomplished something. I had forgotten about this character until some twenty years later when I ran into him at our reunion, and, sure enough, there he was insulting people with his lame jokes. Most of us ignored him just like we did back in school, and it was no surprise to learn that he was twice divorced.

You will not have to take many steps to undermine such a person. Such people hang themselves if given enough rope. Take the high road, and let others take them out. These people are usually not worth the energy required to engage them yourself.

Keep an enemies list, but not for exacting revenge in the way that Richard Nixon did with his list of media and political figures whom he hated. No, we need an enemies list for keeping track of ourselves. If the list is getting too long, it might be time for a self-evaluation.

If you find that you have a lot of enemies, step back and consider your own behavior, honestly examining whether you are at least partly to blame. Just being able to look at yourself objectively is the first sign that you might be alright.

Introspection of this nature does not come easily to chronic enemy makers. They also tend to be no good at truly examining their effect on others. It might be just as well. Those who are not self-aware might be truly horrified if they ever did take a hard, long look at themselves.

Looking in the mirror is not for everybody. Writing this book in a remote West Virginia cabin, I had not looked at myself for several days, because that is how long it had been since I faced the need to present myself to another human. When I was about to meet some friends for a social occasion, I was quite startled at the sight in my mirror. It took some extra time to get cleaned up.

Our personalities can become as disheveled and unappealing as our appearance if we do not get a peek at them now and then. Looking in the mirror at your own behavior and personality is a wise move if you find that people are not responding to you very well.

## USE YOUR ENEMIES WELL

There is something positive about the passions that enemies provoke in us. We cannot become complacent when there is a fight on the horizon, as the novelist Joyce Carol Oates suggests. Enemies prevent us from superficiality, she said.

Look at how Britain and the United States became stronger, economically as well as militarily, in staring down the Nazis during World War II. Indeed, historians will tell you that the Great Depression in the United States was ended largely as a result of the economic engine required to fight the war. Women and African Americans progressed socially and economically as a result of the equalizing effects of war service. That does not mean that we should thank the Nazis—far from it. Many perished by their sword. But once an enemy emerges through no fault of our own, we might as well make the best of it.

Playing high school football, I thought it was interesting that we never played as well scrimmaging on the practice field as we did for a real game against an opposing team. We all gear up more enthusiastically for battle when the stakes are high and an opposing force arises.

Once you have been forced to make enemies, use them well. Harness the anger they provoke as constructively as possible. Still, keep your emotions in check with battling a foe. Like any emotion, anger and hatred are controllable even if they cannot be denied.

## In Dealing with Passive Aggression, Be More Passive and More Aggressive

*The bashful are always aggressive at heart.*
CHARLES HORTON COOLEY

Beware the quiet ones. They can be sneaky. If they are the types who typically get their way by understatement or obfuscation without ever being straightforward about their true wishes or complaints, they might be examples of one of the most challenging personalities in the human race: the passive aggressive.

A passive aggressive comes in many forms, all of them irritating. Generally speaking, they are people who do not say what they mean, do what they say, or ever tell you what they are really thinking.

Not all are quiet. Some will solicit your confidence with grandiose promises of impressive things that they will do for you. But over and over, you discover that they ultimately fail to deliver on the expectations that they had encouraged, instead citing numerous insurmountable obstacles claimed to be beyond their control. If you suspect that they never even intended to do what they promised but were just buying time to win your support, then you might have a passive aggressive on your hands. Whether an underperforming squawker or the sneaky, quiet variety, these types can be a menace in any office, family, or circle of friends.

During my two decades in the journalism field, I have come across several reporters who exhibited passive-aggressive patterns that are found in just about any line of work. They were masters at hustling the boss—their editors, in this case—for choice assignments with big ideas. They would talk about reaching famous sources to quote, collecting unprecedented arrays of data, or finding just the right anecdote to produce an amazing story. Usually, they would buy lots of time to work on this marvelous adventure, all for the hidden purpose of goofing off as long as possible. Throughout the project, they would excitedly brief editors with the next prospect for making the story better, buying even more time to put off filing.

In some cases I never saw the much-hyped story materialize. The sources wouldn't talk. Or the software provided could not properly collate the data. Sometimes another story would come along, distracting everyone, and the original idea would be entirely forgotten. But before long, the reporter would be spinning more ideas to justify not getting any real work done.

A friend of mine describes such people as those who think life is nothing but a dress rehearsal. When it comes time to put the show on the road, they are nowhere to be found.

## PASSIVE AGGRESSIVES ARE SHIFTY TARGETS

Some psychologists consider passive-aggressive behavior a personality disorder. Well put. You will need a tight strategy to tangle with this type. In the reporter's con game described earlier, rarely did I see editors clearly recognize what they were dealing with and take steps to properly manage these people. It is not easy. Passive aggressives are a moving target, skilled at shifting attention away from their failings.

The first step in handling a passive aggressive is to identify the problem. The medical world defines this behavior as someone whose "feelings of aggression are expressed in passive ways as, for example, by stubbornness, sullenness, procrastination, or intentional inefficiency." The term was coined in 1945 by military psychiatrists to describe soldiers who shirked duties with a mixture of passive resistance and grumbling compliance.

A mild, although still irritating, form of this personality type might be a friend or family member who does not want to go to a party but will not say so. Instead, this person takes so long to get dressed for the party that by the time you get there, it is almost over. Many excuses are given for this procrastination, usually, a myriad of obstacles claimed to be beyond the control of the passive aggressive.

These people typically avoid confronting others about problems. They often undermine their targets with comments or actions that, if challenged, can be explained away innocently, dodging blame for their own behavior. They deliberately do a poor job at tasks that they never want to do, but they make sure that something or someone else can be blamed. They might argue against useful suggestions for improving their performance, citing reasonable-sounding excuses for why they cannot implement your ideas.

Once you have identified a passive-aggressive individual who is giving you problems, it will be tempting to confront him or her directly. This probably will not be useful. A hallmark trait of this personality type is that passive aggressives resist all attempts to out their behavior. And one with lots of experience will likely have a lifetime of experience deploying a variety of defenses aimed at throwing doubt on your conclusions: The late partygoer becomes indignant at your suggestion that he or she procrastinated getting dressed because of never wanting to go in the first place. The bills had to be paid, the passive aggressive might say. Do you want the bank to foreclose on the mortgage?

How could you be so unreasonable as to blame the reporter if the promised source refused to talk, delaying or scuttling the story? Even a detailed recitation of a long-standing pattern of underperformance produces a martyred response and a refusal to accept responsibility.

If it is a waste of time to directly confront passive aggressives, what do you do? My answer is to simply fight fire with fire. Be more passive and more aggressive in dealing with them. For example, an editor for the lazy reporter could ask for a review of the interview notes because a story seems so exciting.

Be upbeat and positive in pressuring a passive aggressive; go at them with the same bluster and bullshit that they gave you. And keep it up until the truth of their failures comes out without your ever accusing them of anything.

Giving passive aggressives a dose of their own behavior might get better results than direct confrontation. The next time the party avoider really does want to go somewhere, procrastinate getting dressed yourself.

In most cases, your task is different from that of a mental health expert who is trying to cure the disorder. Either you need to creatively expose the people to get rid of them, or you might simply want to limit the number of times that they pull their stunts on you, and let them bother other people.

Indeed, if you have reason to irritate someone else, try steering the passive-aggressive acquaintance into the target's path and out of your own. You can't be blamed, right? You were just being friendly and helpful—in your own passive, aggressive way.

## PASSIVE AGGRESSION IS NOT JUST FOR PEOPLE

Entire organizations can be passive aggressive. They are friendly places where the people get along without open conflict and manage to reach agreements easily. Everyone working there thinks that things are going along just swimmingly. But the organization goes nowhere, gets very little done, and, if in a profit-dependent environment, might even go out of business or at least limp along, underperforming at every turn. It can happen to a company, a school, a government agency, a church, and even a family. No one seems to know why success eludes the organization because everyone in it is just so darn content.

Well, contentment can be a sign of complacency, the hallmark of an organization that is not asking people to invest their energies, instead allowing them to pretend that great things are being done without actually doing anything particularly great. This phenomenon occurs not so much because the organization is full of underperforming passive aggressives who avoid real and meaningful work, although that is a possible cause. It can happen simply because the organization has no clearly defined goals, few real incentives for genuinely strong performance, or a tendency to shuffle aside creative ideas and promising proposals.

Lines of authority are blurred in passive-aggressive organizations. Those in charge dodge responsibility for results. People are not sure what is expected of them. They go their own way, defining the terms of their participation in the organization however they see fit. It is easy to have a pleasant workplace or a family or community group when everyone is just doing what he or she feels like doing. But, collectively, they are not achieving much of anything.

A family goes days or weeks without dinner together or any discussion about one another's lives. Everyone is living separate lives under the same roof. Everything seems fine because no one is arguing. But that might be because no one is talking to anyone.

People lose touch with one another if they do not take care to routinely nurture the bonds that should be holding them together. My mother calls it *weeding*. Families cannot "let the weeds grow" between them, she says, or sooner or later they cannot even see each other.

The same is true in shared ventures beyond family life. In a company office, everyone just lumbers along seldom even talking as a group about pursuing joint projects or setting goals.

Typically, someone in the organization realizes what a mess things have become and decides that it is time for a retreat or some other dramatic event that will magically bring everyone together. These one-time sessions seldom do any good. If the organization is not weeding on a daily basis, then forget about a retreat or a family vacation changing anything over the long term.

## SHYNESS AS A WEAPON

The American sociologist Charles Horton Cooley had a keen eye for human behavior, as seen in his quote on the bashful being "aggressive at heart." Some people are truly shy, but I suspect that many who give that appearance of being bashful are using it to manipulate others. The shy person can be quite skilled at getting others to do everything for them. "I'm too shy to ask the boss for a raise," a coworker might say, hoping that you get the hint to tell the boss yourself.

Do not fall for the wily ways of the shy. But on the other hand, take a lesson from them. Their techniques are worth borrowing at times. People are often suckers for taking the lead in defense of people who present themselves as being too inferior to take charge.

Consider Scarlett O'Hara, the diva in Margaret Mitchell's epic novel *Gone with the Wind*. Although about as shy and helpless as a speeding freight train, Scarlett is a master at using the appearance of weakness to manipulate men and women. Mitchell's Scarlett is a textbook example of the passive-aggressive operator, but at the end of the book she gets her due when, once more, playing the helpless victim pleading with her husband not to leave her.

Rhett Butler's famous retort could be the model for how to respond to all passive-aggressive people: "Frankly, my dear, I don't give a damn."

## Victory Can Sometimes Be
## Concealed in Compromise

*You win the victory when you yield to friends.*
Sophocles

Compromise is tricky. Give away too much, and you might look foolish to some but generous to others. Give in too little, and you look tough but risk being seen as stubborn or greedy.

Compromise is usually efficient. Sometimes it can be paralyzing. If four drivers come to an intersection, each facing a stop sign, nobody goes anywhere if everyone yields to the other drivers. Somebody has to take the lead. And when he or she does, someone else is usually giving in.

Baseball legend Ty Cobb once called his sport an "unrelenting war of nerves." Such is the rest of life. Hardly a day goes by that we do not negotiate something, large or small.

Standing in line for fast food tends to befuddle me if it is one of those places with no railings or other methods in place for orderly crowd flow. Figuring out where to stand in line is not always clear when there are several registers open with customers wandering from line to line in search of the shortest. Knowing when to yield and when to step forward escapes me. Watching people negotiate this circumstance can be quite revealing about their nature. Some people barge right to the counter acting as if no one else is waiting. These uncompromising types go through life mostly getting their way but annoy lots of people along the way, and, ideally, they pay a price for it now and then. Others hang back, fearful of being rude, and usually end up having a late lunch. These are the wimps who are abused by the noncompromisers.

The intelligent and compromising fast-food customer remains assertive to the jerks and yields to the wimps if they are next, in hopes that everyone gets a turn when he or she deserves it.

## Good Negotiation Avoids Chaos

Negotiations for the rest of life present more-or-less the same dynamic found in the chaos of a disorganized fast-food joint, except that in life at large there is seldom the option of staying in the car and pulling into the drive-through lane where no one can cut in line.

No matter what you are negotiating, you are probably going to need a strategy. First, decide what is the most that you want out of the negotiation, and then consider what is the least that you will accept. Defining your range of acceptance for the outcome should not be left to chance. You might end up with nothing.

Next, try to determine the other person's range of acceptance. If you are buying something, ask for the price right away. If you are selling, immediately ask what the buyer is willing to pay. The first rule of bartering is that the first side to name a price is usually at a disadvantage. That person's range of acceptance is no longer a mystery. Keep yours a mystery as long as possible.

If I am willing to pay $300 for a bicycle and you are willing to sell it for $100, I would be making a big mistake if I am the first to name a price, even if I cut my acceptable number in half. I might end up paying at least $50 more than I had to. Likewise, if you double your acceptable price to $200, you might end up with $100 less than I was actually willing to pay.

Successful compromise, whether selling a bicycle or stopping a war, begins with knowing the other side's true range of acceptance. The most lasting compromise allows both sides to achieve the highest place possible in their range of acceptance. And strong compromise depends on both sides keeping their dignity. If there is a clear winner and a clear loser in a compromise, then it probably will not last.

In the summer of 2006, Israel and Hezbollah reached a tentative compromise that promised to end a weeks-long war between them. In a move that severely endangered the cease-fire negotiations, President George W. Bush declared Israel the winner of this particular war. Even if there really is a winner, few compromises can survive such a declaration.

Worrying about image often blocks the road to compromise. Neither side wants to appear to be the loser, even when one is willing to give in. The quickest path to getting your way, therefore, is to let the other person look like the winner so long as you get what you want. Indeed, pretending to be the loser can help you win much more in most negotiations.

If you want it all—getting your way while making the other person look like a big loser—the odds for success do not favor you in most cases. And even if you do succeed, you might be jeopardizing future negotiations with that person and anyone watching. A reputation for stubbornness does not encourage others to deal with you, leading to missed opportunities.

## How to Win by "Losing"

The ultimate negotiating victory may therefore be in getting what you want while letting the other side think that you caved. There is a good chance that you will give up less than you need to. You see, if the other person is interested in looking like a winner in a compromise, make that person pay for it. Give him or her the perceived victory, but extract a price for it—without making it obvious.

For instance, you are selling your car. I am interested in the car but also want our friends to think that I am a hotshot bargainer. You name an exorbitant price well beyond what you expect. Yes, this might be a case worth violating the rule against being the first to name a price. You do so when you want to start the bidding at a ridiculously high point, allowing plenty of room for the other side to bargain you down to a level that is actually on the high end of your range. The point here is that you are trying to create a scenario in which I look like the toughest bargainer. I counteroffer, perhaps cutting the price in half but still at the upper reaches of what you want.

You accept, making a big spectacle of how you are the big loser and I am a tough-as-nails negotiator. I walk away having paid a premium for the image that I wanted out of the deal. And, here is the nicest part of all: You now have the opportunity to say, "You owe me one." By playing the loser, you might have the chance to get a favor from me down the road—one that you really do not deserve but one that I think I owe you after taking you to the cleaners on the car.

Automotive dealers and other professional sales people often use this ploy, preying on customers who are concerned about looking like a smart negotiator. The pros are adept at quickly figuring out that a buyer wants to impress others with his or her bargaining skills, perhaps a spouse or significant other. Without even realizing, such customers have already put themselves at a disadvantage by showing that image is important to them.

The wise and professional negotiator does not care about image. What difference does image make if you end up with less money for what you sold or if you pay more for what you bought simply because you wanted to walk away looking like the tough guy?

## Give a Little and Gain a Lot

Sophocles was no dummy. Yielding can be the key to victory, he observed. But so many people seem to think that success is all about charging forward in a blaze of glory, mowing down your opponents like Rambo blasting away with an automatic assault rifle in each arm. Such bravado might produce short-term gain but in the long run could win you very little.

Look at the first wave of the Iraq war in 2003. American troops swiftly moved through the country, taking the capital city in short order. But then what? Years later they were under siege, unable to stop what many consider to be a raging civil war. It seemed to be a big mistake early on for the Bush administration to disband and exile the Iraqi military and police forces, many of whom were friendly to the idea of ousting the dictator, Saddam Hussein. By not yielding to these potential friends and, instead, insisting on trying to do it all, the Bush team struggled for years to rebuild the local forces that they had disbanded in order to one day reduce the number of American troops on the ground.

Military planners will tell you that the toughest challenge in warfare is to hold the hard-won ground for the long haul. As in war, you can always achieve a short-term goal if you have overwhelming force that your opponent cannot match. Maintaining your advantage over time is tougher if you have not yielded some of your gains to those who might help you keep control.

## Implement Painful Choices Quickly
## to Minimize the Effects

*Pain is as diverse as man. One suffers as one can.*
Victor Hugo

Being a leader seldom comes without the occasional need to inflict pain. Parents must punish their children when there is no other way to teach a particular lesson. Teachers give bad grades when students deserve them. Bosses fire lousy workers.

Professional politicians constantly face painful choices. In the world of laws and governing, politics is often a zero-sum game because nearly every choice produces a roughly even mix of winners and losers. Just about anytime that a law is passed or a regulation implemented, somebody gains and somebody loses. The trick for the legislator or regulator is to make sure that the losers cannot significantly hurt them in return.

Distributing rewards and punishments can be the very definition of leadership—in government and in the rest of life. If you must make a painful choice, first try your best to avoid taking the blame. Unless you have a reason to show force, why take credit for inflicting pain and risk retaliation against you? If there is anyone handy who stupidly enjoys the appearance of power that comes to those inflicting pain, give the dirty work to that person. You will have made a faithful follower of the one given the task and avoided creating a personal enemy in the one who was hurt. This is why the smart leader of a company seldom does the firing, even if being the driving force behind it. If you think that you need to be seen inflicting pain to be considered powerful, then you surely must be feeling insecure about your power.

After considering whether or how you might avoid blame for a painful decision, try to find an easier alternative to inflicting pain. Or at least make it appear to those on the receiving end that you have searched far and wide for another course, even if you have no desire to find another way. But there are times when pain is unavoidable—from spanking a bad kid to laying off workers to save the company. When pain must come, make it swift. Lingering pain can endanger the pain giver. Companies generally do not keep fired workers hanging around. Not only can they undermine the workplace, but they might steal something. Most companies have security escort them out of the building before they can do any harm.

Prolonged pain also threatens leaders whose followers grow weary of the discomfort. Real physical pain works this way. The sharp but quick pain of a paper cut on your finger might hurt intensely for a second or two, but it eventually subsides, and weeks later you might not even remember it. A mild case of lower back pain might never hurt at any one time as much as the paper cut, but since it never goes away, most of us would gladly trade it for the paper cut.

## DON'T TRY THIS AT HOME

Machiavelli believed that "injuries should be inflicted all at once, for the less they are tasted, the less they offend." He cited an extreme example from ancient Roman history to illustrate this rule. In 317 BC, Sicilian military leader Agathocles decided he wanted to be king of his nation, then known as Syracuse. Instead of waging a lengthy civil war against the government in power, he asked for a meeting with the nation's senate and wealthy elites on the pretense that he wished to discuss an important issue affecting the country. Then, on a prearranged signal, Agathocles had his soldiers kill them all. He was able to seize control without internal opposition from those in power. They were all dead.

Machiavelli's point in citing this example was not to suggest mass murder as a tool for gaining power; rather, he was interested in how Agathocles was able to retain power and "live securely" long after committing such a horrible crime. Machiavelli concluded that by Agathocles's inflicting pain all at once, any negative effects on the rest of his countrymen tended to diminish over time simply because he acted so quickly and completely. A long siege—inflicting the collateral damage on innocents that civil war invariably produces— would probably have left Agathocles much more vulnerable. Machiavelli developed a lesson for new rulers out of this, noting that they must first quickly determine which injuries are necessary in order to gain and hold power.

Machiavelli's conclusion is good advice for any leader who needs to cause pain: "He must inflict them once for all, and not have to renew them every day, and in that way he will be able to set men's minds at rest and win them over to him when he confers benefits."

Cast the pain that you must inflict as positively as you possibly can. Although not always feasible, persuading others that their pain can help them will go a long way toward lessening its effects, reducing the odds that they will hold it against you.

As an employer, my father had to fire workers now and then. He always made the case that it was the best thing for them because they had a better chance of prospering at another company or in another line of work, if they were really awful at their jobs. Although it might sound insincere to some, my father's speech to fired workers seemed to help him avoid making enemies of them.

People are prone to believe that pain can be a good thing, a "learning experience" that "builds character." Tap into this when you are dishing out the pain. As bodybuilders say when they work out, "no pain, no gain."

## Good Cops Can Be Bad

If you have a choice when playing good cop versus bad cop, always try to be the good cop. There is usually somebody around who wants to be seen as the tough guy, expecting that the bad cop gets the power. More often than not, though, the good cop ends up in charge. In most organizations the hatchet man eventually gets axed. I watched this play out in a cabinet-level department during the Clinton administration. The department was targeted for layoffs, and the aide put in charge generated so much ill will among those workers who remained that the aide was fired after doing the dirty work.

Even a Mafia boss who orders a hit keeps some distance from the task. A mere nod to his henchmen or a kiss on the cheek of the intended victim could signal what the boss wants while presenting no clear evidence of his role in the murder. Few crime bosses who ordered hits went to jail for doing so, but plenty of their hitmen were convicted of murder.

Using the murder of opponents as an example of political technique is dicey, I know. And Machiavelli himself was quite conflicted in doing so. It is almost humorous to read Machiavelli's backpedaling in the example that he cited of Agathocles's slaughtering the elites of the country that he wanted to rule. "We can say that cruelty is used well (if it is permissible to talk in this way of what is evil) when it is employed once and for all," Machiavelli wrote.

Throughout *The Prince*, Machiavelli struggles with the immorality of some of his teachings. He well anticipated how these passages would stir controversy across the centuries. But despite the condemnation of his seemingly amoral views, the accuracy of observations on the reality of human behavior became timeless.

Today, millions of American television viewers are entertained by what is basically the modern version of Machiavelli's fictional Prince—the character of Tony Soprano in HBO's *The Sopranos*. In every episode the New Jersey crime boss shows how a true Machiavellian operates with a mixture of cruelty and goodness that, above all, keeps him in power and is—apparently to the television audience of this show—remarkably appealing, despite the ruthless violence. One reason that Tony Soprano is such a popular character is that he actually plays the good guy in most situations, wisely leading his captains, caring for his family, and being aware of his own vulnerabilities. He is an honorable criminal who usually but not always leaves the dirty work to others.

Some television critics have said Tony is a metaphor and a model for less violent leaders in more conventional lines of work. True enough, but he is also the modern extension of the noble leader that Machiavelli created nearly five hundred years ago.

## Suffering Your Way to Success

Those who do not flinch or scream when hurt are said to have "high tolerance for pain." The variety of human responses to pain has been long studied, producing an entire profession within the health industry devoted to pain management.

"One suffers as one can," Victor Hugo said. While perhaps open to several interpretations, this line suggests to me how pain and suffering can be a tool. I recently broke my upper arm, but thanks to the physical therapy, I ended up in better shape than I had been before the accident.

Encouraging a positive outlook on pain will help you ease the harm that you must occasionally do to another. Whether punishing a child, firing an employee, or failing a student, cast the experience as character building. Remind the pain receivers that they would not be the people they are today without painful growing experiences. Tell them they are lucky—it could be so much worse!

## Distribute Rewards Slowly
to Prolong the Effects

*The reward of a thing well done is to have done it.*
RALPH WALDO EMERSON

$A$sk people if they want the good news or the bad news first, and most choose to get the bad news out of the way. They want to save—and savor—the good news for last.

It is tough to enjoy the good news if you have no idea just how bad the bad news might be. It might turn out to be not as bad as you have imagined, making the good news that much sweeter. The same goes for distributing rewards and punishments. Better to get your punishment all at once and get it over with. But as much as we might want our rewards all at once, the smart distributor of rewards metes them out as slowly as possible to prolong the beneficial effects and thus maintain the faithful following of the one on the receiving end.

If you need to motivate a child to improve grades, develop a reward system on a timetable so that you prolong the anticipation and enjoyment of the rewards. The same goes for bonuses and other benefits at the office. Machiavelli wrote, "Benefits should be distributed a bit at a time in order that they may be savored fully."

Airlines and hotel chains perfected the art of managing reward distribution with their frequent-traveler programs. Built on a system of collecting points for travel that you pay for, these programs promise the delayed reward of free travel once you have earned sufficient points. Frequent-traveler rewards created a near-riot in the marketplace. For some, gaming the point system became an addiction. A friend of mine once booked a day of travel on an airline, ending the trip where it began, just to collect the remaining points needed for a free ticket.

Travel companies were also gaming the customers. They skillfully designed the timetables for earning rewards, making it take just long enough to get the freebies so that the company did not have to give away too much but short enough so that the customers believed that it was worthwhile to spend the bulk of their traveling dollars chasing the rewards that the company was offering. By prolonging the effects of reward distribution, the companies gained millions of loyal customers.

Distributing rewards gives you control of the best kind. Your followers remain faithful because they like what you do for them and not because they fear what you might do to them. The latter also brings control but the kind that also makes enemies along the way.

When distributing rewards, be sure to get the credit. Handing out punishment usually should be delegated to others, but the smart leader makes sure to take responsibility for handing out rewards.

## The Lost Ideal of Sacrifice for Future Gain

It is getting tougher for bosses, parents, teachers, and other leaders to manage reward distribution. Society demands more rewards than ever these days.

Teachers at all levels see this. I recently asked a high school teacher to name the most significant change in student behavior over the twenty-five years that she had been working with students. She immediately replied that today's students and their parents expect good grades whether deserved or not. "They think they should get a good grade just for showing up," she said.

College educators I have met report the same phenomenon. One told me that he has a stock reply for the growing ranks of students who insist that they deserve a higher grade on a paper or an essay exam. "I tell them I'll be glad to re-grade it, but I cannot guarantee that I won't decide to lower the grade," he said. With that line, this professor finds that most students decide to accept the initial grade.

Employers report that young workers today expect their rewards up front before they have earned them. Many expect immediate promotions, raises, travel perks, and anything else that employees used to wait years to receive. I once had a worker ask to take paid vacation in the first month on the job.

Old sayings like "good things come to those who wait" are no longer part of our culture. We want everything now. The microwave oven takes too long for some people.

Baby boomers are getting much of the blame for this. The offspring of World War II parents, they grew up with more wealth and privilege than that of any generation in human history. And it appears that they are teaching their children to impatiently expect the good life without much effort.

This will be a tough generation for leaders to handle. In government, elected officials face impatient voters who want immediate results and lots of benefits. Employers are dealing with a workforce that no longer values a system of delayed gratification that must actually be earned.

Establishing a merit-based distribution of gradual rewards is one of the toughest challenges that today's leaders face. The first step is in understanding the need to introduce the concept to growing numbers of potential followers who have not been conditioned to work long and hard for their rewards.

## THE FREEDOM OF FORGOING REWARDS

The fewer rewards you need in life, the more freedom you will have. Consider the attitude of the Buddhist monk who had only one possession, a pan. As he was climbing a mountain, the pan fell from where he had tied it to his side and plunged down a hill beyond reach. The monk instantly kneeled and gave thanks for finally being freed of the burdens of possession.

The monk was a bit extreme, to be sure, but rewards are like possessions. They come with burdens as well as pleasure. Some cost-benefit analysis might be in order. Is the reward of a better title at work worth the aggravation if it does not come with a pay increase? When your member of Congress proudly announces a federal highway grant, is it worth getting the new local road if your taxes go up to cover the costs of this and a thousand other pork projects around the country? Rewards are often used by others as a tool to win favor, but they can come with hidden costs. A child gets candy for being good but ends up with a stomachache.

View those offering rewards with suspicion. But how tempting it can be to play the fool in hopes of a big payoff. State lotteries are built on this. The miniscule odds of winning deter few people from plunking down their hard-earned money for the remote possibility of getting rich. Even those who win lotteries sometimes seem cursed by their newfound wealth, encountering burdens and difficulties that they never imagined when chasing their dream. You have to wonder if some would return the money to reclaim their past life.

Does it make me a lazy bum that I decided in law school that maintaining grades above a C average was too much work? My campus was so close to the beach that the cost-benefit analysis argued in favor of more time in the sun. There was such a vast difference between the amount of work required for a middling performance and that of a superior showing.

Perhaps I am lazy, but I thoroughly enjoyed my law school experience—even though it kept me out of the ranks of the higher-paying law firms. Still today, I try to make only enough money to pay for the things that I really want. To me, struggling to make more is not worth it—what it would buy I can live without.

Choosing how much reward you need in life should not be lightly considered. Chasing rewards simply for the sake of winning them might not be such a happy choice.

Take stock of the happiest people you know. Are they rich, poor, or in the middle? My guess is that you will discover the happiest people to be those who have a touch of that Buddhist monk's attitude. Sometimes it pays to be thankful for what you do not have.

## THE JOY OF INTANGIBLE REWARDS

We cannot all be as content and philosophical as Ralph Waldo Emerson, but he offered a worthy ideal in suggesting that accomplishment is reward enough. It makes for a nice twist of the slogan in the Nike commercial: "Just do it."

Sometimes just doing something is enough. When that happens, how sweet it is. To be honest, I make very little money writing books. While it would be nice to make more, I am satisfied with the sense of achievement.

Long ago I struck upon a concept that I found to be very helpful whenever the physical rewards of an endeavor were outweighed by the pure enjoyment of doing it: psychic income. We are so conditioned in life to measure success and happiness in such tangible ways the size of a paycheck or the square footage of our homes—but very often we can be just as fulfilled with less tangible rewards. Be satisfied with no more than purely psychic income for some efforts, and you might find life much more enjoyable.

## Allowing Others to Speak Truthfully Diminishes Their Respect for You

*Even better than respect is obedience.*

CHINESE PROVERB

Knowing when to tell painful truths is a tough challenge for followers. Knowing when to listen to bad news is a hard choice for leaders. Relations between leaders and followers often fall apart when the truth is not well handled. In most cases it is safer to tell people in authority only what they want to hear. There is no risk of retaliation. It is tempting to flatter a powerful person to gain their confidence and support.

But Machiavelli was no fan of flatterers. He devoted an entire chapter of *The Prince* to counseling distrust of them: "How Flatterers Must Be Shunned." The wise leader needs to hear more truth and less flattery, he believed. "Men are so happily absorbed in their own affairs and indulge in such self-deception that it is not difficult for them to fall victim to this plague," Machiavelli wrote. "The only way to safeguard yourself against flatterers is by letting people understand you are not offended by the truth."

Still, Machiavelli warned against letting everyone around you tell the truth. He advised a "middle way" of choosing a small circle of wise counselors who are free to tell you things that you might not want to hear. But if you allow all to speak truthfully, you risk losing their respect for you, Machiavelli concluded. This advice is not limited to Machiavelli's target audience, the rulers of nations. Anyone in a leadership position faces the question of when to hear only what one wants to hear and when to listen to advice that one might not prefer to hear.

Surround yourself only with flatterers, and you could be vulnerable to unexpected developments that harm you. But let all of your subjects complain to you or criticize your decisions, and you risk being seen as a weak leader, losing the respect that maintains your power.

## AUTHORITARIANS ARE POLITICAL FAILURES

Authoritarian leaders often end up in failure because they built a world of illusion around them, refusing to accept advice or let anyone tell them what was really going on. An extreme example would be Adolph Hitler still barking out field orders to his generals from the confines of his bunker in Berlin, seemingly oblivious to the fact there was no more army to command. And even then, the sycophants around him fed the illusion, pretending to follow his orders.

Weak leaders accept too much advice. An aide to Senator John Kerry's presidential campaign in 2004 told me that the Massachusetts Democrat listened to so many people that he devised a trick for the best way to influence him. The aide simply waited until everyone else had spoken, sometimes even until the senator was in the hallway after leaving the meeting, and then he would give his opinion. "He usually took the advice of the last person to talk to him," this aide explained.

Those who serve a leader must likewise examine the always-tricky question of how and when to tell the truth. Is your boss the type of person who holds bad news against you or the type who wants to hear about problems so that they can be intelligently solved? You must find the correct answer to these questions to maintain secure relations.

Just as the leader must find Machiavelli's middle way, balancing flatterers and truth tellers among his circle of advisers, those who serve a leader must also seek a middle ground. Flatter the boss on occasion but not so often or so grandly that it does not seem genuine. If a tough decision went particularly well, say so.

Professional flattery is safer than personal flattery in most cases. Praise management skill, not clothing choices, for instance. Personal flattery might not come across as genuine in the context of the workplace. It could earn you a reputation for being a suck-up. The occasional kind word for how the leader leads could be more appropriate and better received. But underlings who look to be evaluating the boss can also give the appearance that they ought to be the one in charge—that, but for a fluke, they would be and should be the CEO. Many bosses find this offensive.

Flattery is easy compared to finding the right way to tell those in authority something that they might prefer to avoid. Start by showing empathy and appreciation for the burdens of their position. "It must be tough to be the one who has to hear about everybody's problems," you might say before unloading your own problem case.

Tread lightly when communicating painful truths to a superior, especially if you have not done so before and have not yet learned how this person processes such information. Reveal your information incrementally, carefully measuring the response with each step. Watch for body language, even the twitch of an eyebrow, that might indicate resistance to what you are saying. Abandon course if it seems that you are not deemed worthy of saying such things. Better to hint at the problem that you want to address, in hopes that you will be asked questions for more detail, a telling sign that you might be allowed to speak truthfully. Take care to identify solutions for every problem that you describe to someone in authority. By focusing on solutions, your identification of a problem seems less negative.

If you value your relations with a leader, do not gain a reputation as a flattering suck-up or as a whining problem-monger. A strong leader avoids both types. But, of course, if you are dealing with someone who wants to hear only good things, then flatter away. Just don't count on this person to stay in power for a very long time.

## Don't Count On Permission to Speak Freely

You are not guaranteed safety even when a superior appears to accept your constructive criticism. Be quite sure of your safety before speaking further, despite the apparent receptivity. This is not an easy thing to determine. All the signs of a positive response could be evident, and your honesty might still backfire on you. Some people take the advice of those who offer honest criticism and then cut the critics out of their lives.

I have had bosses who profusely thanked me for being truthful, only to discover that they did not appreciate it at all. This taught me to keep my mouth shut, a hard lesson often learned the hard way. I knew someone at one organization who believed to be getting ahead with blunt observations at meetings. That person was eventually no longer invited to the meetings.

Bureaucracies, by their nature, tend not to encourage people to rise above the din and offer honest appraisals or bright ideas. It happens in corporations as well as government agencies. A strong organization that fulfills its mission should welcome ideas and criticism, but such outfits seem to be quite rare.

Retaliation against criticism is not limited to targeting what people say or do on official turf. This has become a side effect of the dramatic expansion of the numbers of people going on the Internet to write their own journals, called *blogs*. Employees are getting fired for criticizing the company in their personal blogs. Some have been fired for engaging in activity on the Internet that the company deems inappropriate, even if that activity is unrelated to the business where the employee works.

Journalists, despite working in a profession that thrives on freedom of speech, are losing their jobs for going on blogs to give their own opinions about public matters, even when they do so under a fictitious name.

E-mail at the office is also a dangerous place to say what you think. Most workers probably understand by now that the company owns the e-mail system that they use at work and, consequently, has the legal right to read anything that you write to anyone—which makes e-mail, even to someone off-site, the worst place to vent your feelings about the office. A good rule is to never put anything in an e-mail that you would not say directly to the boss or whomever you are writing about.

## THE RELATIVITY OF OBEDIENCE

Chinese proverbs seldom miss the mark, and the one advising obedience over respect is worth following. You do not have to respect a superior to at least pretend to be obedient and get your way. Even if you know for an absolute fact that you are being ordered to do something incredibly stupid, you might be better off making a lame effort to comply than to immediately resist.

A story about Michelangelo offers a clue to surviving a ridiculous command. When presenting a sculpture to his benefactors, a group of church officials, one of them complained that the nose on his subject was too large and ordered him to make it smaller. I am sure that the great master was tempted to plunge his scalpel into that priest's heart, but instead he discreetly gathered some dust in one hand, climbed to the top, and, while simulating the sound of scraping the marble, dropped some of the shavings he had carried with him. In truth, Michelangelo had not touched the sculpture, but the unknowing church officials deemed his supposed revision a grand improvement and accepted the piece.

That sculpture became one of history's greatest works of art, the statue of David—and also a testimony to the success of false obedience.

## Never Postpone Inevitable Conflict

*I am at peace with God.*
*My conflict is with Man.*
CHARLIE CHAPLIN

$T$ry not to shoot at anything that can shoot back. But do not hesitate to shoot if you are about to get shot. If the fight is inevitable, better to join the fight than wait until your foe has more ammunition.

Most conflicts can and should be avoided. But every now and then an unavoidable one comes along. Knowing the difference between unnecessary hostilities and inevitable conflict takes a lot of practice. Look back on your own tussles in life and consider how many of them now seem insignificant and avoidable. For those fights that you believe could never have been avoided, think about what made them so and apply this standard when faced with future disagreements. Identifying a conflict that cannot be postponed starts with determining that it cannot possibly be avoided.

Regularly scan your social and professional surroundings for signs of troublemakers, those who might provoke serious conflict down the road without a preemptive strike. This could be someone new at work who seems a bit too eager to do your job. Or you may meet someone who shows too much interest in your significant other.

Early spotting of inevitable conflict allows you to respond incrementally. You have the option of gradually escalating hostilities until the threat is removed, never using more force than necessary. "Nip it in the bud," the saying goes. Failing to act early enough could increase the likelihood of a rapid unmanageable escalation. Machiavelli wrote, "One should never allow chaos to develop in order to avoid going to war."

There is great danger in miscalculating the inevitability of conflict. If you strike unnecessarily, you end up with a war that you could have avoided. And no matter how prepared you might be, war of any kind—between nations or people— can take unexpected turns against you.

President George W. Bush provoked a lot of anger around the world and at home when his administration justified the 2003 invasion of Iraq as a "preemptive strike" against the threat of weapons of mass destruction being used against the United States or its allies. Had the threat been real or provable, Bush's preemptive strike doctrine would have fared better as time went by. But as it turned out, the Bush administration was never able to prove its equation that conflict with Iraq was inevitable. The supposed weapons of mass destruction never materialized, at least not to the extent originally claimed.

Bush and his war team lost credibility due to their miscalculations about the Iraqi threat. The American public eventually began telling pollsters that the whole thing was a mistake.

## Preemptive Strikes Need Special Care

The preemptive strike doctrine makes sense in a war against terror if the potential threat can be proven. And it makes sense in the rest of life, whenever unavoidable conflict looms. But how much force do you apply when an early strike seems necessary?

Incremental escalation of hostilities is usually best. If a coworker poaches on your turf, drop a subtle hint that you've noticed the incursion. If that doesn't produce a retreat, up the ante by making it clear that not only have you noticed but you really care. Keep raising the temperature until the threat is removed. Going too far at first, such as running to the boss to complain, will leave you with few options for further escalations.

Some people are simply bent and determined to make trouble. They thrive on conflict and seem to relish aggravating others. A timetable of incremental escalation against them might prove to be fruitless. Follow it anyway. It is important for others to see you as the more reasonable party and to see the aggressor as the bad guy. And so long as you are applying gradual force, you will not be seen as a weak victim.

Turning the other cheek, as Jesus prescribed, might be advisable for conflicts that do not matter so much. Some people taunt others just to test them, to find the limits of what they will take. Keep them in the dark by waiting to show you care until you really have no choice. Conflict purely for the sake of conflict benefits neither side. Everybody loses unless someone has something to gain from the conflict.

Cherokee Indian philosophy managed a proper balance between peace and war. As someone with a smidgen of Cherokee blood, I have long studied Cherokee ways. Primarily a peace-loving people, they nevertheless remained prepared for war, becoming adept at making weapons of war but only using them when they had no choice. They kept in place a precise system for organizing themselves when war with another tribe or invading Europeans became necessary. Once war threatened, a war chief took over the Cherokee government, and the entire society pursued victory with all determination.

The Cherokee approach to conflict is a good one for modern life. Never seek it unnecessarily, but prepare well for it and know exactly what to do when it comes.

## Postpone Avoidable Conflict

Teddy Roosevelt's philosophy "Speak softly and carry a big stick" seemingly echoes the Cherokee way of thinking about conflict. But Roosevelt was not as soft-spoken as his philosophy would have us believe. And I dare say that most people who quote his famous line do not follow it to the letter as much as he did. Those who admire Roosevelt's big-stick maxim tend to skip over the part about speaking softly and instead use the stick when doing the former might get the job done.

The Rough Rider projected American power around the world in ways that were entirely new for the young nation that he commanded. He thrived on conflict, whether hunting animals or trying to subdue nations in the neighboring Southern Hemisphere. Until Roosevelt's era the United States had remained mostly isolated from the rest of the planet. America has embarked on many wars since Roosevelt dreamed of making the country a major force in the world. As also happens in relations between people, the United States fared best in those conflicts that were inevitable, when facing a foe that provoked an unavoidable war. World Wars I and II were such conflicts. Wars fought by choice did not end with clear American victories. In Vietnam, Korea, and Iraq, the outcomes were murky at best.

Determining to be tough and to never shy away from inevitable conflict is not an excuse to fight when hostilities might actually be avoidable. Knowing the difference between inevitable and avoidable war is the hallmark of wise leadership in any setting. No matter how wise or foolish it is to engage the enemy in combat, make sure that you aim well and hit your target. A wounded foe is far more dangerous than one you never shot at.

Hunting wild hogs in Florida's Ocala National Forest as an eleven-year-old, I learned just how frightening a wounded animal can be compared to one that you leave alone. Before I had drawn a sure bead on this hog, I fired anyway, grazing my prey's leg instead of killing him. He wheeled around and, baring those menacing fanglike teeth, charged with full and furious force straight toward me. I was paralyzed with fear. Thankfully, my dad was on hand to shoot that crazed beast down just a few feet before he got to me.

From then on, I did not shoot a hog unless I had a clear shot to make the kill.

### Humans Are the Most Violent Species

Engaging in conflict seems to be human nature. Animals coexist better than we do, even though they eat each other. At least they do not raise armies and ravage everything in sight.

Charlie Chaplin had his share of "conflict with man," as he said. The talented moviemaker fought studio moguls as well as the moral authorities of his day. Taking his quote to a broader level, it could be said that all of humankind's conflict is with the rest of humankind.

Human beings are the most violent species on the planet. On any given day, do an accounting of all the living things that you have killed—for the leather in your furniture, the meat in your refrigerator, and a long list of other "necessities." Only humans commit murder, if defined as killing for profit, revenge, or hatred. Only humans start wars or commit genocide. The rest of Earth's species are quite tame by comparison, killing for food and survival.

We need not beat ourselves up for our nature but rather control the worst of it and hope for the best while being realistic that we cannot always avoid a fight. If anything, remaining peaceful at all times is against our nature.

Living a life without conflict is just not in the cards for anyone. Pretending otherwise could leave you unprepared and therefore vulnerable. Somebody somewhere will take advantage. Even the most pacifist person should be ready to fight back.

# The Powerful Never Give Up Control; It Must Be Taken Away

*I love power.*
NAPOLEON BONAPARTE

If you want even a fraction of someone else's power, do not expect that person to give it to you. Eve had no illusions that her actress mentor, Margo, would ever share the stage with her in the film *All about Eve*. So she took her chance when she got it.

But as often happens when the powerful are challenged, Bette Davis's Margot gave Eve a "bumpy night" when she discovered her protégé's treachery. Eve learned a lesson about taking what you want from others. As Jimmy Durante said, "Be good to the people you meet on the way up; they're the same people you meet on the way down."

Have no illusions about the human passion for power. Those who depend on raw power for control will never give it up. They must cling to it, or they have nothing. If you must have their power, you must take it. But remember, if you take power from others, so it might be taken from you someday. Lord Acton said it best in his famous line "Power tends to corrupt and absolute power corrupts absolutely."

How do you identify a control freak? It is a phrase often used in jest to tease one who is trying to micromanage the lives of others. While benign in most cases, a genuinely power-mad person in your life—especially, one who has authority over you—can be an obstacle to your own success. There are telling signs of a power freak who must be challenged, circumvented, co-opted, or completely avoided if you are going to survive in his or her midst. Sound the alert in your head whenever you encounter someone who demands blind obedience, sets forth impossible tasks for others to perform, or demonstrates an unrealistic bias for simple solutions that probably do not even make sense.

Sound familiar? Chances are, you have run into this personality type at least once in your life. These people are everywhere. They can be family members, friends, bosses, politicians, and celebrities. Anyone exhibiting such traits probably is a full-blown power freak.

Failure to obey is not an option for players in the power freak's world. The powerful often seek to dehumanize those around them to control them. They see others as tools or toys exclusively placed on Earth for the purpose of servitude. Lucky for them, there are plenty of insecure people in the world who thrive on submitting to a powerful person's will.

The impossible task is a favorite ploy of the powerful. They gain more control by setting you up to fail. It gives them superiority to make a spectacle of your failure, allowing them to frighten their other subjects with public admonishments.

Unrealistically simple solutions appeal to power freaks because they tend to believe that everyone else is stupid and unable to see the easy answers that they do. To them, sorting through the nuances of a complex problem is nothing but a sign of weakness.

Those who jealously protect their power often project supreme confidence, but in truth they are probably afraid, perhaps even painfully insecure at heart. This makes them vulnerable to a more psychologically secure challenger who can exhibit genuine confidence to the following.

### How to Handle a Power Freak

How do you deal with uncontrollable power freaks in your life? For starters, you could run away. Complete avoidance is the best policy wherever it is feasible. But if you must engage them, be prepared to completely undermine them. Remember the rule: The powerful never give up power; it must be taken away.

It is tempting to make alliances with a more powerful person. But rarely do you find a chance to share power with that person. Machiavelli advised never to "become the ally of a more powerful" person. If you win your shared goal, you become this person's "prisoner," and it is better to avoid "being in other men's power," he wrote.

To gain your own power, you will have to set about undermining the more powerful person in every way. There are many insidious techniques for doing so. Direct confrontation is a bad idea in most cases. Someone more powerful automatically has the advantage. It is far better to undermine a powerful obstacle in your life by indirect means.

Start by encouraging the more powerful person's weaknesses. Most power freaks love flattery. By all means, flatter away. Nudge them even further into the illusory world in which they live, making them all the more vulnerable to painful truths that they cannot see.

Feed the power freak's delusion of intelligence. Power freaks are not always as smart as they might seem. If they were, they would do a better job of protecting their power by becoming strong leaders who make wise decisions and encourage willing followers based on well-earned faith instead of blind obedience.

Pretend to be obedient to the power freaks. Make them think that you wake up every morning thinking of better ways to serve them. Enlist others in your project but always without saying what you are up to. When an impossible task comes along, for instance, steer it to someone else.

Feed the power freak's need for simple solutions. Develop an arsenal of famous sayings or management rules to cite. Never give the power freak complicated or lengthy analyses of issues.

The more that you gain the power freaks' confidence, the better positioned you will be to take advantage of them when the time comes. And if you have accurately identified a power freak as someone who holds power in all the wrong ways, the time will come when his or her power can be taken away.

## Control Your Inner Freak

Too much micromanagement of others can be your downfall. For many of us, it is unavoidably difficult to give up control and let people do things even just a bit differently from the way that we want something done.

Loosening your control does not always mean giving up power. Indeed, it can give you more power. People often view wise delegation as a sign of power. It also helps prevent mutiny against your power. Give your followers some owner-ship of their duties, and they will probably take more inter-est, be more creative, and even more faithfully accept your leadership.

Let go, and sometimes you might find that variations of what you expect are not so awful. They might even lead to better results. When that happens, say so. Acknowledging that your employee, your child, or someone else on your watch came up with a better solution than yours will likely earn you that person's respect.

Constantly nagging others to do everything your way can be a morale killer. Focus on results, not methods. So long as people end up in the right place, often it is best to let them find their own way. If riding in the car with a friend, do you insist on managing the route to your destination? Even if your plan might be a few minutes faster, getting into a dis-pute about it is probably not worth the effort. And who knows, it is always possible that your friend can get there quicker than you think.

Ultimately, being a control freak is just plain narrow-minded. It closes the door to unexpected options that can lead to better results. Impose too many strict rules on peo-ple, and they might just walk away—or worse, they might conspire to undermine your power.

You have to wonder if Martha Stewart might have avoided jail time if not for the friends and business associates who turned on her when she went to trial for lying to investiga-tors about her stock dealings. She was partly undone—in the courts of law and public opinion—by the poor character references from those who had experienced her famously controlling nature.

Being a strong leader often means showing others the right path without belaboring the dos and don'ts. One of my law professors had a secret for keeping clients that can apply to leaders who want to keep their power: Don't lecture them on "what they can and cannot do," he said. "Advise them on how to do what they want to do."

## Power Is a Tool, Not a Toy

Napoleon ended in exile because he wanted power for the sake of being powerful. A popular myth holds that, because he was short, he needed power to be a big man. Today we look at such people and say that they have a "Napoleon complex." But standing at 5 feet, 6 inches, Napoleon was actually of average height for men of his day—proving that a Napoleon power complex is not just for short people.

No matter how physically short or tall you might be, if you use your power for only yourself, do not expect to have it for long. Power should not be a plaything for your own amusement. It should be a tool for the good of you and your followers. The more who benefit from your power, the longer you will have it. Keep it to yourself, and it will soon be gone.

Leaders in any arena stay on top by serving the people who follow them. Those who want it the other way around provoke resentment and unhappiness that will haunt them when the followers turn against them. The best way for leaders to keep long-term power is to make their followers' dreams come true.

# INDEX

Acton, Lord, 150

*Aesop's Fables*, 49

Agathocles, 128, 130

Alexander the Great, 76

*All about Eve* (film), 150; self-importance, dissection of in, 63

Allen, Woody, 31, 36

ambition: control, loss of, 29; as dangerous, 25; as drug-like, 26; limits, defining of, 27; and politics, 25

American Dream, 30

American presidency: and "followship," 70; and promises, 70, 71

Andersen, Hans Christian, 77

*The Andy Griffith Show* (television series): leadership on, 94

Arkansas, 46, 47

arrogance, 62, 64, 65; as attitude, 66; as self-defeating, 63

*The Art of War* (Sun Tzu), 34

authoritarianism: resistance toward, 80

automobile industry, 30

baby boomers, 134, 135

Barnum, P. T., 21

Balzac, Honoré de, 94, 99

Beard, Charles A., 62, 67

*Being There* (Kosinski), 19

Berra, Yogi, 12

blogs, 142

Bonaparte, Napoleon, 150, 155

Bono, Sonny, 32

Bremer, L. Paul, 34

Brennan, Walter, 58

bureaucracies: criticism in, 142; followers in, 79

Burr, Aaron, 9

Bush, George H. W., 47, 105

Bush, George W., 6, 15, 55, 105, 122; administration of, 125; and change, 33; compassionate conservatism, call for, 92–93; and fear, 16, 17; and Iraq War, 33; as politically isolated, 7; preemptive strike doctrine of, 145;

Caesar, Julius, 78, 79

captology, 90

Carter, Jimmy: on lying, 44–45

Castro, Fidel, 78
Central Intelligence Agency
  (CIA), 78
change: as entertaining, 91;
  and flexibility, 31, 32–33;
  middle ground, as safe, 92;
  as necessary, 88; and originality, 39; and repetition,
  91, 92; resistance toward,
  89, 90; success, as hallmark
  of, 33; techniques for, 89,
  91; as upsetting, 87, 92
Chaplin, Charlie, 144, 149
Cheney, Dick: as hatchet man,
  57; spotlight, avoidance of,
  56; as workhorse, 55
Cher, 31, 32
Cherokee Indians: conflict,
  approach to, 146–47
Church Committee, 78
Church, Frank, 78
Churchill, Winston, 6
Civil Rights Act, 17–18
Clairol, 37
Clinton, Bill, 93, 105; administration of, 129; broken
  promises of, 46, 47; empathy of, 102, 103; and
  Lewinsky affair, 8, 9, 24;
  as moderate, 92; and taxes,
  20, 21
Clinton, Hillary, 8, 29
Cobb, Ty, 120
codependency, 104, 105; and
  power, 100
Colson, Charles, 13
compromise: as efficient, 120;
  image, as obstacle, 122,
  124; as tricky, 120; victory,

and yielding, 124. *See also*
  negotiation
conflict, 146; avoidance of, 144;
  and human nature, 148,
  149; inevitability of, 145;
  and leadership, 148; preparation for, 147
control, 51; and ambition, 29;
  as basic need, 1; battle for, 1;
  and control freaks, 4; as dis-
  appointing, 2; and favors,
  81; and fear, 13, 14; and love,
  13, 14; and moderation, 88;
  need for, 3; and playing politics, 5, 6; and politics, ix, 5;
  and power, 4, 150; and rewards, 14, 133; as unachievable, 2; victim, role of, 11;
  weakness, as effective, 11
control freaks, 151; as narrow-
  minded, 154. *See also* control, power; power freaks
Cooley, Charles Horton,3, 4; on
  bashfulness, 113, 119; and
  "looking glass self," 3
Cooley, Mason, 87, 92, 93
Crawford, Joan, 76
curiosity, 51

Davis, Bette, 63, 64, 150
Dean, Howard, 69
Deaver, Michael, 103
DeLay, Tom: reputation of, 56;
  as show horse, 56
democracy: definition of, 74
denials, 10
dependency: cultivation of,
  101, 102; as economic, 101;
  power politics, as essential,

100; in power relationships, 105, 106

Disney, Walt, 54

Disraeli, Benjamin, 49, 54

Douglas, Stephen, 20

Dukakis, Olympia, 58

Durante, Jimmy, 150

Duvall, Robert, 58

Eagles, 104

Einstein, Albert: insanity, definition of, 34

e-mail: at office, 142, 143

Emancipation Proclamation, 20

Emerson, Ralph Waldo: on rewards, 132, 137

empathy: and followers, 102

enemies, 96, 110; as savior, 107; and self-awareness, 111; temper, losing of with, 108, 109

enemies list, 110, 111

Enron, 26, 46

equivocation: and gossip, 10; as weakness, sign of, 9

familiarity: as comforting, 38

favors, 86; as business transaction, 82; control, diminishing of, 81; as dangerous, 81; good relations, maintaining of, 83, 84, 85; and rewards, 136

fear: as motivator, 13, 14; punishment, dread of, 14

*A Few Good Men* (film), 21

flattery: and leaders, 138; and power freaks, 152; professional vs. personal, 140

followers: in bureaucracies, 79; and empathy, 102; and "fol-

lowship," 69, 101; and groups, 72, 75, 76; individuality, shunning of, 72; leaders, choosing of, 100; leaders, codependency between, 70; and loyalty, 75; and order, 101; and truth, 138, 141 following, 73; building of, 71; dissent, punishment of, 71

force: and persuasion, 49

Fromm, Erich, 100, 105

Frost, Robert, 12

Gabriel, Peter, 104

Gandhi, 25, 87

Germany, 69

Gibson, Mel, 11

Goldberg, Whoopi, 58

Goldwater, Barry, 15

*Gone with the Wind* (Mitchell), 119

Gore, Al, 57, 105

Great Britain, 112

Great Depression, 15, 112

Great Society, 18

greed, 26

Guyana, 69

Henley, Don, 104

Hezbollah, 122

Hitler, Adolph, 6, 25, 69

Hugo, Victor: on suffering, 126, 131

human nature, 50, 57; and conflict, 148, 149; as violent, 149

humility: benefits of, 85–86

Hussein, Saddam, 125; mistakes of, 97–98, 99

imitation, 39, 42
indecision: dislike of, 12
introspection, 3
Iran, 45
Iraq, 97; invasion of, 65, 145
Iraq War, 33, 124, 148
Israel, 122

Jesus, 3
Johnson, Lyndon, 13, 17–18,
    101; civil rights legislation
    of, 74
Jones, Jim, 69
Jones, Tommy Lee, 58
Jonestown massacre, 69

Kennedy, John F., 15
Kerry, John F., 16, 57, 139; as
    flip-flopper, reputation of,
    44
*King of the Hill* (television pro-
    gram), 70
King, Martin Luther, Jr., 87
Korean War, 148
Koresh, David, 100–1
Kosinski, Jerzy, 19

Landau, Martin, 58
lawmakers: types of, 55
leaders: and appearance, 76;
    as authoritarian, failure of,
    139; dependency, cultiva-
    tion of, 101; as flexible, 31;
    followers, codependency
    between, 70; and listening,
    138; and moral behavior, 78;
    pain, infliction of, 126, 127;
    rewards, distributing of,

133, 135; and rivals, 79;
    as weak, 139. *See also*
    leadership
leadership, 73; and conflict,
    148; definition of, 126;
    essence of, 72; and evil, 77.
    *See also* leaders
Leno, Jay, xi
Lewinsky, Monica, 8, 9, 24
Lincoln, Abraham, 20, 43, 48;
    on silence, 53
Lincoln-Douglas debates, 20
Livius, Titus, 81, 85–86
lying, 21, 44, 45; as calculated,
    20; as experts, 22, 23; and
    hypocrisy, 22; manipula-
    tion, of others, as tool in,
    22; social bargain of, 19;
    and "white lies," 22

Machiavelli, Niccolo, ix, x, 3,
    20, 21, 55, 57, 131; on ambi-
    tion, 25; on appearance,
    76; on arrogance, 67;
    on benefits, 132–33; on
    change, 31; on conflict, 145;
    as cynical, 50, 51; on fear,
    14, 15; on flatterers, 138; on
    hatred, 68; on imitation,
    37, 42; on leadership,
    morality of, 77, 78; on love,
    14; on middle way, 138–39,
    140; on pain, 128; power,
    techniques of, 52; on pow-
    erful, 152; on promises,
    making of, 43; on rivals,
    78–79; teachings, immoral-
    ity of, 130

McCain, John: campaign finance reform, 88
Michelangelo, 143
Mitchell, Margaret, 119
moderation, 87; and control, 88; status quo, advantage of, 89

negotiation: and losing, 123; and strategy, 121. *See also* compromise
Newman, Paul, 58
Nicaragua, 45
Nicholson, Jack, 21
*1984* (Orwell), 17
Nixon, Richard, 15, 110; arrogance of, 67; demise of, 67; Imperial Presidency of, 13; as vulnerable, 14

Oates, Joyce Carol: on enemies, 107, 111
obedience: as false, 143; and respect, 138, 143
originality: and change, 39; dangers of, 38, 39; and idea thieves, 40, 41; in workplace, 39
Orwell, George, 17

pain: infliction of, 126, 127; and leadership, 126, 127; as learning experience, 129; responses to, 131; as swift, 127, 128. *See also* pain management
pain management, 131. *See also* pain

passive aggressive personality: as challenging, 113; confrontation, avoidance of, 115; handling of, 116; in organizations, 117, 118; patterns of, 114; as personality disorder, 114; responsibility, refusal of, 116; as term, 115
persuasion: and computer technology, 91; and force, 49
political skill: as dangerous, 6
politics, x; as absolute, 5; and ambition, 25; and control, ix, 5, 6; essence of, ix; playing of, 5, 6; and war, 109
positive reinforcement, 14
power, 56; as action, 99; and codependency, 100; conservation of, 99; and control, 4, 150; and delegation, 153–54; dependency, as narcotic of, 100; desire of, 95; dissipation of, 57, 60; and enemies, 96, 107, 108, 109, 110; and enemies list, 110, 111; and followers, 60; gaining of, 152; and generosity, 97; and God, 58, 59; humiliation, use of, 151; and insecurity, 152; as invisible, 59; lessons of, 98; maintaining of, 95; and moderation, 87; mystery of, 59; and rivals, 78, 79; seeking of, 95, 96; and self-awareness,

111; as tool, 155; and trust,
46; and truth, 45; under-
mining of, 152; use of, 57,
60, 61; as visible, 59, 99;
and vulnerability, 152;
wanting, vs. obtaining, 94;
power freaks: flattery, love of,
152; handling of, 152, 153.
*See also* control; control
freaks; power
power plays, 96; and reverse
psychology, 96–97
preemptive strike doctrine,
145, 146. *See also* Bush,
George W.
*The Prince* (Machiavelli), x, 68,
138; Tony Soprano, character of, 130
promises: as broken, 44, 46,
47; as illusory, 43
public opinion, 74
punishment: and fear, 14

al Qaeda, 16, 64
Quayle, Dan, 105

Reagan, Ronald, 15, 45; empathy of, 102, 103
reality-based television, x
respect: and obedience, 138,
143
rewards, 132; and accomplishment, 137; and Casual Friday, 14; and control, 14, 133;
and delayed gratification,
135; demanding of, 134; favors, winning of, 136; and
freedom, 135; and psychic

income, 137; and student
behavior, 134
reward system, 14, 132; and
frequent-traveler pro-
grams, 133
rigidity: as enemy, 36
Roman Empire, 99
Roosevelt, Franklin D., 16
Roosevelt, Theodore, 17; big-
stick maxim of, 147
Rove, Karl, 16
Ryan, Meg, 37, 38

Santa Claus, 22
self-awareness, 3, 4, 111
Sellers, Peter, 19
September 11 attacks, 15, 16, 64
Sheen, Fulton J., 69, 74
shyness: and manipulation, 119
silence: use of, 53; as weapon,
52
*The Simpsons* (television series), 79
Sinatra, Frank, 58
slavery, 20
Sophocles, 120, 124
Soprano, Tony: popularity of,
131; and *The Prince*, 130
*The Sopranos* (television series),
130
state lotteries, 136
Stewart. Martha, 154–55
Sting, 104
strategy, 36
Streep, Meryl, 58
strength: playing to, 35; and
weakness, 34, 35
Sun Tzu, 34, 35

*Survivor* (television program), x

terrorism, 64, 65
*Thelma and Louise* (film), 34
*Thunderdome* (film), 75
*The Tonight Show* (television program), xi
trust: and power, 46
truth, 22, 24; and power, 45
Twain, Mark, 77; and truth, 22
Tyson, Mike, 11

United States, 97, 112, 145; arrogance of, 64; isolation of, 147; September 11 attacks on, 64; wars of, 148

Van Halen, 103
Vanna White syndrome, 53
video games: and warfare, 91

Vietnam War, 148
Voltaire: on imitation, 37, 42

Walt Disney World, 54
war, 107, 108, 125; and enemies, 109; and politics, 109
Washington, George, 62
Watergate, 14
weakness, 34, 108; acknowledging of, 35; and strength, 35
*Wheel of Fortune* (television show), 53
*When Harry Met Sally* (film), 37
White, Vanna, 53
Wilde, Oscar, 19, 24, 75, 80
World War I, 148
World War II, 112, 148

Young, Andrew, 55, 60

## About the Author

**Craig Crawford** is one of Washington's most popular commentators. He has been hailed by the *Washington Post* as "one of the capital's most celebrated journalists." His wit and wisdom are featured almost daily on national television and radio programs, including *The Early Show* on CBS; various programs on CNBC and MSNBC, such as *Countdown with Keith Olbermann* and *Hardball*; and CBS Network radio. A White House columnist for *Congressional Quarterly*, he is a frequent commentator for NBC's *Nightly News*, CBS's *Evening News*, and *Imus in the Morning*. Before joining *Congressional Quarterly*, Crawford ran *The Hotline*, an online news digest that is an institution inside the Beltway and out. Before coming to Washington, Crawford practiced law in Florida and was a reporter for the *Orlando Sentinel*. He lives in Washington, D.C.